THE CRISIS OF LABOUR

INDUSTRIAL RELATIONS & THE STATE
IN CONTEMPORARY BRITAIN

THE CRISIS OF LABOUR

INDUSTRIAL RELATIONS & THE STATE IN CONTEMPORARY BRITAIN

David Coates

University of Leeds

Philip Allan
OXFORD AND NEW JERSEY

First published 1989 by

PHILIP ALLAN PUBLISHERS LIMITED
MARKET PLACE
DEDDINGTON
OXFORD OX5 4SE (UK)

and

171 FIRST AVENUE
ATLANTIC HIGHLANDS
NEW JERSEY 07716 (USA)

British Library Cataloguing in Publication Data
Coates, David
  The crisis of labour: Industrial relations and the state in contemporary
  Britain.
  1. Great Britain. Industrial relations. Policies of government 1951–1988
  I. Title
  331'.0941

  ISBN 0–86003–407–0
  ISBN 0–86003–707–X Pbk

Library of Congress Cataloging-in-Publication Data
Coates, David.
  The crisis of labour: industrial relations and the state in contemporary
  Britain/by David Coates.
      p. cm.
  Bibliography: p.
  Includes index.
  ISBN 0–86003–407–0.
  ISBN 0–86003–707–X (pbk.)
  1. Industrial relations—Great Britain.
  2. Industrial relations – Political aspects—Great Britain.
  3. Industrial relations – Government policy—Great Britain.
  I. Title.
  HD8391.C57 1989
  331'.0941—dc 19
                                                              88–31704
                                                                   CIP

Typeset by DMD Ltd, St Clements, Oxford
Printed and bound in Great Britain at the Alden Press, Oxford

To Robert and Edna Coates
Emma, Ben and Anna
Thomas and Edward
with love

Contents

Preface

In writing this book, I have benefited from conversations over the years with Bob Looker, with colleagues at the University of Leeds, and more recently with new colleagues in the Social Science faculty at the Open University. My debt to all of them is considerable, and it is pleasant to be able to acknowledge it here. In the preparation of the manuscript, Thomas and Edward helped to draw up the bibliography, Richard Hyman read an early draft of Chapters 2 to 5, and so too did my brother Barrie. Ed Brown and other colleagues at an international conference in Holte, Denmark, commented on a later version of Chapter 5; John Hillard helped with the proofs; and Penny Muter read the entire manuscript with her usual sense of detail and perspective. I am grateful to all of them—and particularly to Barrie and Penny—for the advice they gave and for the care with which they gave it; and though none of them holds any direct responsibility for the argument to come, each is responsible for the fact that the argument is more accurate and more nuanced than it would otherwise have been. I want to say too how much I have benefited down the years from the support of my parents and from the love of my children. It is to them that I would like to dedicate this book.

David Coates
University of Leeds
October 1988

1

The Crisis of Labour

The chapters that follow trace a story: of the changing relationship of workers, unions, political parties and the State in the United Kingdom since 1951. Their main initial purpose is to *lay out* the key features of that relationship, and to *explain* why and how those features have changed.

This exercise should be of interest to a number of audiences. First, it should make a contribution to the work of two sets of students: those of industrial relations and those of contemporary British politics. Traditionally, the literature and concerns of these two disciplines within the social sciences have been rather different. Students of industrial relations have been encouraged to concentrate upon questions of job regulation, and to focus their work primarily on rule-making processes associated with the organisation of work. Industrial relations has been a subject that people have studied from the *factory up*: looking at work practices, at structures of managerial decision making, and at the role of forces seen as 'external' to the factory—at trade unions, at industry-wide agencies, and eventually at the State. Students of politics, on the other hand, with their interest in rule-making processes of a more public kind, have been encouraged to start with the State, and then go *down*: to look briefly at the private institutions (such as unions and management) which lie beyond the State. They have been encouraged to approach non-state agencies as parts of civil society, as 'external' to the State, as interest groups, coming in to shape the outcome of public processes of policy making that have their own well-established history and legitimacy.

This division of focus has always been constricting, and distorting to a degree. It is a particularly limiting and inappropriate one now because, for nearly three decades, the *politics of industrial relations* have been central *both* to public policy *and* to the private world of industrial bargaining. After all, it is nearly thirty years since Selwyn Lloyd, as Chancellor of the Exchequer, launched his 'pay pause'. It is over twenty years since Harold Wilson's bitter confrontation with the 'politically motivated men' of the National Union of Seamen. So students of both industrial relations and contemporary British politics do need a clear 'map' of what has linked the differing subject matter of their respective disciplines in recent times; and they do need some sense of why that 'map' has come into existence in the form that it has. A literature on this, of course, already exists; and the chapters that follow must be seen as a contribution to that literature.

One reason for supplementing an already existing literature lies in the connection between the politics of industrial relations and a second audience: one concerned with the state of the Left in Britain. A debate is currently in progress—in and around the Labour Party—on the prospects for socialist politics in contemporary Britain. In one sense, this debate is an old one—one that has gone on in different forms ever since organised labour movements emerged to challenge capitalism in the last half of the nineteenth century. But it is a debate which has gathered renewed urgency in Britain of late, because of the Labour Party's heavy defeat in three successive general elections. The chapters that follow contribute to that debate.

They do so in a number of ways. At the personal level, they enable me to revisit and revise earlier contributions of my own to the more esoteric and academic end of the longer debate, as the notes in the text will periodically show. But more immediately and more importantly, they constitute an attempt to move the focus of the more recent discussion away from its conventional concerns with policy, personality and immediate electoral success. It is commonly accepted on the Left in Britain that the entire socialist project here faces a serious crisis of programme, support and confidence. The temptation of the moment, for practising politicians at least, is to seek a resolution of that crisis in limited adjustments to manifestos, minor changes of personnel, and strenuous revampings of image. But as presumably even they recognise, the crisis of the British Left has deeper roots than that; and the recognition of those roots is a vital pre-requisite to any long-term revival in left-wing fortunes here. The chapters that follow offer an examination of those roots.

This book is therefore both a survey and an argument. It is a survey of the interplay of industrial relations and politics in Britain since 1951; and it is an argument about the crisis of labour which is at the heart of that interplay. What the chapters do is to tell the story of the relative tranquillity of the relationship between managers and workers, and between both and the State, in the years of steady economic growth and rising living standards after 1951. They then trace the disintegration of that tranquillity as the post-war settlement between capital and labour on which it rested slowly came unstuck. They show how first a Labour Party, and then a Conservative Party, response to that disintegration brought a politicisation of industrial relations, and with it a series of bitter confrontations between well-organised groups of workers on the one side, and entrenched and powerful governments on the other. And they show, too, that the inadequacy of those responses, and the severity of those confrontations, have combined to make essential a wholly new kind of political involvement in industrial relations in the 1990s.

The chapters will argue that there has been, and there still remains, *a crisis of labour* in industrial relations and politics in contemporary Britain, a crisis of labour that will go away only with the creation of a democratic and socialist society and economy in this country. In the absence of such a society in the years since 1951, the crisis of labour has taken a number of different but inter-related forms. It emerged *first* as a crisis of labour for capital, a slowly emerging recognition of the problems caused for private capital accumulation in Britain by the industrial strength of organised workers in the years of full employment after 1945. That industrial strength then precipitated a *second* crisis of labour—a crisis this time for the Labour Party to whom organised workers in the 1950s and 1960s gave their electoral support—a crisis occasioned by the Labour Party's inability to harness that industrial power for radical political ends. Labour in power after 1964, and again a decade later, turned the authority of the State against the industrial might of its own working class base, and in the process seriously eroded its electoral relationship with it. This second crisis of Labour—this emerging tension between the industrial and political wings of a hitherto united labour movement —then laid the ground for a *third and final* crisis: a crisis of organised labour itself, as Thatcher governments capitalised on the failures of their Labour predecessor, and used state power to erode the capacity of workers to organise and unions to grow. It is to resolve these three crises that a new politics of industrial relations is now required, one that links the industrial power of workers to a radicalised Labour Government able to roll back the defeats imposed on organised labour by Conservative governments and strident employers in the Thatcher years.

The chapters that follow examine in turn the different phases of the crisis of labour. Chapters 2 and 3 look at the emergence of the crisis in its first form. Chapter 4 looks at it in its second, and Chapter 5 in its third. Chapter 6 then offers one set of thoughts about how to put the crisis behind us.

2

The 'Golden Age' of Industrial Relations

If we had been writing this study of industrial relations and its politics thirty years ago, both the tone and the content of the text to come would have been significantly different. For both when viewed from the more troubled vantage point of the late 1980s, and when seen by contemporaries against a backcloth of interwar depression, the whole climate of industrial relations in the 1950s seems particularly serene. Mass unemployment had gone, apparently for ever. Work was available for virtually all who sought it, and the job security enjoyed by those in work was high, and seemed permanent. In the immediate post-war years unemployment levels were very low. The rate of unemployment in 1945 was 1.2%. Fifteen years later, in 1960, it was still only 1.7%; and between those two dates the highest point it ever reached was 3.1% in 1947, 'a year marked by an acutely bad winter which affected production very adversely' (Coates 1982, p.175). Otherwise, unemployment crossed 2% in only 4 years out of the 15 up to 1960, kept down throughout by the temporary resilience of 'old' industries and by the rapid expansion of new ones.

I

Until the late 1950s many of the industries which had dominated the interwar economy, like coal, were still booming under the demands of post-war reconstruction; and even those which were not, like cotton, were only at the beginning of a period of orderly decline whose impact on their participants would later be softened by government assistance and the availability of work elsewhere. The very rapid shrinkage of employment in these old industries— in cotton, coal, shipbuilding and railways—was still to come; and in the 1950s, even before it occurred, it was obvious that new industries were expanding rapidly (such as light engineering and motor vehicle construction) and that large numbers of new jobs were being created (in the offices of big private companies and in the welfare bureaucracies of the State). As the decade opened, 14,450,000 men and women were employed as manual workers, and only 6,948,000 as white collar. By 1961 white collar employment had risen to 8,478,000, while employment in manual work had declined to 14,022,000. And by then, jobs in the new industries (motor vehicles and engineering, chemicals and the bureaucracies of the State) had expanded to total 4.8 million. The full figures of occupational change for the 1950s are given in Table 2.1.

Table 2.1   The Occupied Population of Great Britain, by Major Occupational Groups, 1951–66

Occupational groups	Numbers in thousands		
	1951	1961	1966
Employers and proprietors	1117	1139	832
White collar workers	6948	8478	9461
(a) Managers and administrators	1245	1268	1514
(b) Higher professionals	435	718	829
(c) Lower professionals and technicians	1059	1418	1604
(d) Foremen and inspectors	590	682	736
(e) Clerks	2341	2994	3262
(f) Salesmen and shop assistants	1278	1398	1516
Manual workers	14450	14022	14393
(a) Skilled	5617	5981	5857
(b) Semi-skilled	6124	6004	6437
(c) Unskilled	2709	2037	2099
Total occupied population	22515	23639	24686

Source: George Bain *et al.* (1972, p.113) 'The labour force', in A.H. Halsey (ed.) *Trends in British Society Since 1900* (Macmillan).

The relative serenity of industrial relations in Britain in the 1950s was not just a product of full employment. It was also in part a consequence of the kinds of products then being created for the first time by that fully employed labour force. For the industries and state hierarchies which absorbed so much new labour in the 1950s were geared to the generation of a set of wage goods and a range of social services which had hitherto either not been available at all, or whose consumption before the war had been generally restricted to a privileged minority. State employees were charged with the provision of extended education, health care and pensions for the entire population; while the new manufacturing industries generated an ever-growing volume of consumer durables, from vacuum cleaners to cars. The dissemination of these began to seep steadily down the social hierarchy in the 1950s. Not, of course, that many workers had cars or foreign holidays then. That was to come—for skilled workers anyway—20 years later. But already vacuum cleaners, televisions and fridges were becoming available to wider and wider sections of the employed population as living standards, though still low, steadily began to rise. It was, after all, only during the 1950s that the annual wage rise became the accepted norm, and that the pattern of industrial relations between managers and managed eased, as 'real wages grew by more than a quarter 1950–65, with an increase in every year except 1962' (Ackrill 1987, p.230).

In retrospect, the precarious nature of this new prosperity, and its dependence on highly contingent and soon-to-be-threatened bases, is all too obvious. But it was not so obvious at the time. Contemporary commentators—both on politics and on industrial relations—were united in their sense of permanent change and improvement. They were struck in particular—in the realm of the political—by the way in which, in most advanced capitalist countries, trade unions had acquired new powers and status. They were struck too by the electoral victories of Labour and social democratic parties, and by the fact that the welfare systems created by labour parties in power were not later dismantled by incoming governments of the right. Unexpected developments of this kind, accompanied as they were by an unprecedentedly sustained period of economic growth, led political sociologists like Seymour Martin Lipset to treat the 1950s as a qualitatively new era in Western politics. Lipset spoke for an entire generation of liberal scholarship when he announced in 1960 that:

> The fundamental political problems of the industrial revolution have been solved: the workers have achieved industrial and political citizenship; the conservatives have accepted the welfare state; and the democratic left has recognised that an increase in overall state power carries with it more dangers to freedom than solutions to economic problems. This very triumph of the democratic social revolution in the West ends domestic politics for those intellectuals who must have ideologies or utopias to motivate them to political action.   (Lipset 1960, p.406)

Such a faith in the 'end of ideology' was mirrored in the literature on industrial relations by a belief in the permanent diminution of industrial disputes—and that, too, was tied to the growing status and power of trade unionism in the wider community. Professor B.C. Roberts, for example, discussing 'what was believed in the 1950s to be an established feature of Britain's industrial relations—the virtual disappearance, since 1926, of the large-scale strike as an official instrument of union policy' (Fox 1985, p.369), said this in 1957:

> The reluctance of the unions to use the strike as a means of enforcing wage demands is a marked feature of the rise in their status . . . Whichever party is in power, the trade unions are consulted about every measure that affects them. They are represented on no fewer than sixty governmental committees and have access to Ministers at almost any time they desire . . . The British trade union leader of today considers himself to be a responsible industrial statesman: his status is assured and he is ready to accept responsibility with pride.
> (B.C. Roberts, cited in Fox 1985, p.369)

What neither Professor Roberts nor, in the more general context, Seymour Martin Lipset, allowed for was the actual basis of 1950s prosperity. They were conscious of the existence of that basis, of course. They just characterised it in a particular, and ultimately inadequate, way. This was certainly the case with Seymour Martin Lipset, who presented the economic revival and political stability of Western Europe and the United States in the late 1950s as the product of an economic order that was no longer capitalist in any traditional Marxist sense of that term. Lipset was by no means alone in arguing this. Many American liberal scholars interpreted economic and political developments in the 1950s in a similar way. So, too, did many revisionist intellectuals within the British Labour Party. Anthony Crosland, for example, in his widely read book *The Future of Socialism*, put a similar case. Writing in 1956, and surveying the changes in Britain produced by the policies of the 1945–51 Attlee Government, Crosland posed the rhetorical question, 'Is this still capitalism?' and replied, 'I would answer "No"' (Crosland 1956, p.42).

In fact, the economic and social order that he and Seymour Martin Lipset surveyed was still capitalist in the traditional Marxist sense. Production was still controlled by a class of capital owners, and profits were still extracted by them only through the systematic exploitation of the labour power of a proletariat denied the ownership and control of its means of production. What Anthony Crosland saw as a new social order, others have more properly and more recently seen as a stage of development *within* capitalism itself—a stage variously labelled as 'Late Capitalism' or 'State Monopoly Capitalism': one dominated by Keynesian-inspired politics at home and by American military and economic power abroad. Since neither Keynesian policies nor American power have turned out to be without their problems, the timeless statements and unbounded optimism of Cold War liberal scholarship has more recently been forced to retreat in the face of a harsher and more conflictual world (for Anthony Crosland's own retreat, see his *Socialism Now*, 1974). For this reason, the demise of Keynesianism, and the decline of American power, will be vital elements in our later discussion of the crisis of Labourism and the rise of a revitalised Conservative Party. What we have to establish first, however, is the earlier arrival and consolidation of these now challenged bases of the post-war world order, and their impact on industrial relations in Britain in the years *before* monetarism appeared and mass unemployment returned. It is with the establishment of the character of industrial relations in Britain during the first half of the long post-war boom that the rest of this chapter is therefore concerned.

II

The local domestic source of this new context of industrial relations in the 1950s was the political settlement made between capital, labour, and the State during the Second World War, which was enshrined in the post-war government commitment to full employment and the welfare state. This post-war settlement was a direct product of changes in the balance of power between classes, and of alterations in popular attitudes and expectations created by the war effort itself. The wartime mobilisation of labour had brought full employment back to British factories and had shifted the balance of class power towards organised work groups in British manufacturing industry. With labour in short supply, it simply was no longer possible for managers or politicians to discipline workers by threatening them with unemployment. Instead, their co-operation had to be won, and retained, by the recognition of their institutions (most notably trade unions), by negotiations with their representatives (often shop stewards), and by the provision of improved rates of pay.

Moreover, the war involved both civilians, and civilians as soldiers, in a massive collective endeavour which was presented and understood as a defence of democracy against fascism. Yet if large numbers of people were to risk their lives defending that democracy, and were to go on risking their lives year by year in its defence, they had to believe that what they were fighting for was in reality worth defending. They could hardly be expected to die just to defend the right of their kind to be without a job, a decent house, or enough food and clothing for themselves and their loved ones. Their parents had fallen for that package in 1914, and the trick was unlikely to work twice. So, during the war, politicians came to realise (some more quickly than others, Churchill slower than most) that the prospect of a post-war return to 1930s scale unemployment and mass poverty could not sustain the popular defence on which the British State and Empire depended for its survival. Only the prospect of a better society, with jobs and prosperity for all, could inspire and justify the scale of popular sacrifice required in the fight against fascism; and the realisation of that came to dominate the war-time discussions of plans for post-war reconstruction. As each year of hostilities gave way to the next, pressure built up for the creation, after the war, of a fairer and more socially egalitarian Britain, one in which the State would provide at least minimum levels of basic welfare for all. As James Cronin put it, the experience of war 'created a broader public consensus on the shape of post-war society. It nudged political discourse to the left, and made Keynesian economics and state intervention acceptable to "middle opinion" and to the bulk of the electorate' (Cronin 1984, p.112).

This shift to the left was also reinforced, after 1941, by Britain's alliance with the Soviet Union, which made it temporarily impossible for ruling groups in the West to attack industrial militants and discredit left-wing forces, by their usual strategy of strident anti-communism. The shift to the left manifested itself politically during the war in popular support for the Common Wealth party, for the Beveridge Report, for the 1944 Education Act, and for the coalition government commitment to full employment. This crucial promise of full employment was enshrined in the White Paper 'Employment Policy' published in May 1944. It committed post-war governments of either party to having 'as one of their primary aims and responsibilities the maintenance of a high and stable level of employment after the war' and to using government policies, including public expenditure, to influence demand to achieve this (Barnes and Reid 1980, p.12). It was this commitment more than any other which was guaranteed by the fact, and by the scale, of the Labour Party victory in 1945. For that victory quite simply took from the immediate agenda of post-war British politics any possibility of a quick return to the non-interventionist policies of inter-war Conservative governments.

What the post-war settlement enshrined was in part a set of policies, to which we will turn in detail in a moment; but it also enshrined a set of relationships between politicians, senior trade union leaders and leading industrialists whose character is important to our argument here. As we have just observed, the commitment to full employment totally altered the balance of power between classes, and in particular obliged politicians to 'manage' rather than to 'ignore' trade union pressure and working class concerns. The Labour politicians who held sway between 1945 and 1951 were keen to do this in any case; and their Conservative successors, 'after six years in opposition and with a slim majority . . . were not inclined to challenge the deduction that to manage the economy successfully required the consent of both sides of industry' (Middlemas 1979, pp.405–6). So Conservative governments in the 1950s continued to allow full play to what Middlemas called 'the corporatist bias' in national British politics, avoiding any 'open and public break with producer groups' and conceding instead that 'such organised groups had a "right" to take part in making policy: indeed that their approval of a relevant policy or programme (was) a substantial reason for public confidence in it' (Beer, quoted in Middlemas 1979, p.407). As a result, and under the terms of the post-war settlement, the unions 'crossed the political threshold, and became part of the extended state' (*ibid*, p.373). They became, that is, what Middlemas also called 'governing institutions, existing thereafter as estates of the realm, committed to co-operation with the state, even if they retained the customary habit of opposition to specific party governments' (p.372). Government policy in its turn succumbed to a 'cult of equilibrium', proceeding only with the balanced support and agreement of peak organisations of capital and labour, and as a result moving only incrementally in one direction or the other.

The policies around which both sets of representative institutions (capital and labour) cohered were underpinned by the general adoption—at the highest levels of the British State in the late 1940s—of Keynesian ways of analysing the workings of a national economy. There is now a considerable debate in the literature on post-war British politics about whether, and to what extent, there ever was a full-blown 'Keynesian revolution' in Britain. (On this, see Barberis 1987.) The details of that debate need not concern us; but its existence serves as a reminder that Keynesianism was, at best, only part of the post-war British story. But it was a part, and a vital one at that: particularly, though not exclusively, for the Labour Party. For Keynes's ideas gave Labour a way of bringing its mild anti-capitalism into line with its need to generate jobs and prosperity from an economy that was in all its essentials still a capitalist one. Keynesianism offered Labour politicians a set of policies that could—under special circumstances at least—flush nearly full employment out of an economy still riven with class divisions, owned by a tiny section of the population, and based on the pursuit of private profit. Since none of that had seemed possible to many socialist theorists of the inter-war years, the Labour Party before the war had been offered only a paralysing choice between a revolutionary upheaval for which it had no desire and an unmanaged capitalism over which it had no control. The arrival of Keynesianism created—and was perceived as creating, as early as the 1930s, by the intellectuals who would lead the post-Attlee labour movement—a middle way between private capitalism and state socialism; and because this was so, the Labour Party leadership at national level after 1948 progressively took Keynesianism to be its creed, its project, its solution to the old dilemma of how to run and reform capitalism simultaneously. As Adam Przeworski has commented:

> It was Keynesianism that provided the ideological and political foundations for the compromise of capitalist democracy. Keynesianism held out the prospect that the State could reconcile the private ownership of the means of production with democratic management of the economy. . . . Keynesianism provided the foundation for class compromise by supplying those political parties representing workers with a justification for holding office within capitalist societies . . . Keynesianism suddenly provided working class political parties with a reason to be in office. It appeared that there was something to be done, that the economy was not moving according to natural laws, that economic crises could be attenuated and the waste of resources and the suffering alleviated if the state pursued anticyclical policies of demand management . . . The government had the capacity to close the 'full employment gap' to insure that there would be no unemployment of men and machines. Full employment became a realistic goal that could be pursued at all times. (Przeworski 1985, pp.207–9)

Thus Keynesianism is important to any analysis of the politics of contemporary industrial relations for two distinct but related reasons. It is important because of its centrality to that post-war settlement between capital, labour and the State which was guaranteed by the electoral victory of the Labour Party in 1945. Keynesianism is important too because of the way in which the post-war Labour Party, far more even than its Conservative opponents, came to rely on Keynesian ideas to guide its entire political project, and to shape the detail of its relationship with both private industry and the trade union movement. For that second reason, as we will see in detail later, it makes sense to understand the crisis of Keynesianism in the 1970s as primarily a crisis for the Labour Party in British politics: a crisis which touched the Conservatives of course, but which did not traumatise and immobilise them, as it has Labour. But in the 1940s that was all far away, unseeable and unanticipated. By 1945 Keynesianism was available to direct the manner of economic intervention of the post-war British State; and was used for that purpose, both by the Labour administration and by the Conservative ones which followed.

John Maynard Keynes was a Liberal, a supporter of Lloyd George, and a critic of what he called 'unregulated capitalism'. In direct opposition to inter-war economic orthodoxy, he argued that the unemployment of the 1930s could not be solved by restricting government spending and cutting wages, as the Treasury appeared to believe. It was true, he conceded, that cutting the price of a good (in this case, wages as the price of labour) should increase the good's consumption (that is, bolster employment). That, after all, was the Treasury view, that unemployment rates had their own natural rhythm which could only be exacerbated by well-meaning but ultimately misguided state plans to hold wages higher than the market would allow. The Keynesian critique of such passivity before the market found part of its intellectual rationale in the observation that wages were a rather special kind of price. They were not only a cost of production: they were also a source of demand. To cut them was to reduce the purchasing power that firms needed if they were to realise their profits through the sale of the commodities they generated from the employment of labour. To cut wages (and hence purchasing power) would actually lower business confidence, and with it investment and employment. In the conditions of the 1930s, Keynes argued, the system required more demand and more spending, not less demand and more saving; and that could best be generated, he thought, both by redistributing income from the high savers (the rich) to the low savers (the poor), and by the government spending more money itself, generating a multiplier effect through the whole economy by an expansion of its own labour force, and by its purchasing of the products of the private sector.

What Keynes advocated were cautious and well-controlled 'anti-cyclical policies, allowing deficits to finance productive public works during depressions and paying back the debt during periods of expansion' (Przeworski 1985, p.36)—what he termed a 'somewhat comprehensive socialisation of investment' (Keynes 1936, p.363). On this argument, 'the state became transformed almost overnight', from 'the passive victim of economic cycles' to 'an institution by which society could regulate crises to maintain full employment' (Przeworski 1985, p.36). On this argument too, workers' demands for higher wages suddenly 'gathered a universalistic status'. No longer a threat to general prosperity via their pressure on profits and investment, 'a higher total wage fund reappeared as the necessary trigger to greater Aggregate Demand, profitability and employment' (ibid., p.37). The Keynesian specification for the role of the State that emerged in the 1930s was one which required the government to manage levels of demand in the economy as a whole (by its instructions to banks, and by its own spending) in order to keep demand at a level which would generate high levels of employment. Keynes himself was quite cautious on how high 'high' could be without inflation setting in; some of his followers were less so. Full employment itself became a possibility, and indirect demand management by the State held the key to its achievement.

In reality, such Keynesian initiatives worked only because of the underlying productive capacity of the post-war capitalist economies, and because of the manner of their reconstruction in the critical years after 1945. After all, there was little new in the popular aspiration for a better world after war. That aspiration— of a land fit for heroes—had been evident in 1918 too; but governments in the 1920s had failed to deliver such a new social order because of the very different balance of class forces (both domestically and internationally), and the very different conditions of capital accumulation with which their economies had been faced. The weight of the American economy, and the role of the American State, had been crucial in 1918, as it was to be in 1945. In 1918 the Wilson initiative to rebuild Europe on a liberal– democratic and capitalist basis had failed initially through American isolationism, but eventually (in 1929) through the collapse of the American economy occasioned by the very severity of the defeats imposed on American workers in the 1920s. Lacking the purchasing power to sustain rapid capital accumulation, the American economy, too, had succumbed in 1929 to severe depression from which it had emerged only on the basis of the renewed industrial militancy of American unions in the 1930s and the subsequent mass mobilisation of the American labour force for global war. As Mike Davis has written of patterns of class power in America after 1918:

> during the first great consumer-durable boom of the 1920s, the majority of the semi-skilled industrial working class remained trapped in poverty-level incomes, unable to participate in the hoopla of car and house buying. In this sense, incipient Fordism (i.e. mass consumer-led economic growth) was defeated by the very success of the open-door 'American plan' which destroyed unionism and blocked wage advance. It took the decade-long struggle of the new industrial unions to force the way for union recognition and the codification of a dynamic wage system—in the collective bargaining agreements of the late 1940s—to synchronise mass consumption to labour productivity (and) in this fashion (to raise) perhaps a quarter of the US population—especially ethnic-white semi-skilled workers and their families . . . to previously middle class and skilled worker norms of house ownership and credit purchase during the 1950s.   (Davis 1987, pp.10–11)

By 1945 American capital was in a much stronger position than it had been in 1918 to fuel a generalised economic recovery throughout the capitalist bloc. Its leading manufacturing firms faced an internal market sustained by extensive price-tied wage agreements, and they possessed a revitalised industrial capacity in need of peacetime (and overseas) outlets for its products. They also possessed a state élite who were prepared to create the bloc-wide conditions in which rapid capital accumulation could again flourish. This was achieved through initiatives by first the Truman and then the Eisenhower administrations. These administrations lent Marshall Aid to Western Europe, tied all Western European currencies to the dollar in the agreement at Bretton Woods in 1944, ran a vast balance of payments deficit in dollars to sustain huge American armies in Europe, and encouraged American capital to invest abroad. New semi-automated industrial systems which had developed during the war (in the motor vehicle, chemical, and light engineering sectors) were there for deployment across the entire western capitalist bloc, to provide the rapid increase in labour productivity on which, for two decades, profits could rise and wages grow simultaneously. The only threat to this American-inspired capitalist revival came in the 1940s from the industrial militancy and political radicalism of revitalised labour movements. But this was in the event blocked: by a mixture of intense anti-communism after 1948, by the incorporation of non-communist trade union leaders and social democratic parties into a pro-American alliance, by the systematic defeat of major industrial disputes in Japan, West Germany and France, and by the exploitation of the vast reservoirs of available factory labour to be found in Western Europe's displaced persons and over-populated countryside.

It is worth emphasising the degree to which the post-war boom depended on what Leo Panitch has called:

> this combination of special conditions . . . the cleansing of unproductive and less dynamic capitals during the depression and the war; large post-war pools of skilled cheap labour; clusters of technological innovation favouring productivity growth and mass consumer demand; the weakening of trade union militancy during the Cold War; the abundance of cheap raw materials and the availability of new markets and relatively open trade under United States economic leadership.   (Panitch 1986, p.6)

The emphasis is important here because, by the 1970s, as we will see, most of those conditions had gone; and in their going, the politics of industrial relations in Britain were transformed. But while these special conditions survived, they generated twenty-five years of sustained economic growth and expanding world trade, and gave to white male workers in the capitalist bloc as a whole a degree of generalised prosperity and harmonious industrial relations for which there was no obvious precedent or parallel in capitalism's entire history. The figures for economic growth in the capitalist bloc as a whole are given in Table 2.2.

Table 2.2 Economic Growth, 1950–70 (annual percentage rate)

	1950–5	1955–60	1960–5	1965–70
OECD	5.7	3.9	5.9	6.0
USA	5.0	2.4	5.8	4.8
EEC	8.2	6.7	5.6	6.5
Japan	18.0	16.0	11.6	16.5
UK	3.5	2.3	3.2	2.0

Source: M. Barratt Brown (1972, p.101).

As the table makes clear, even the British economy, weakening in competitive terms though it had been since the 1890s, was able, in the space created by this American-supervised post-war expansion, to experience its longest and most sustained period of industrial growth. In fact, successive British governments locked themselves into a secondary supporting role to the United States in the policing of this new post-war American empire. British troops stood East of Suez, sterling operated as a second reserve currency to the much-wanted but initially very scarce dollar, and the City reconstituted itself as a major financial centre. The long-term costs of that subordination—and in particular the opportunities missed to modernise British industrial capital before the re-emergence of West German and Japanese competition—would return to haunt British governments in the 1960s and 1970s, and to transform the context of industrial relations in the process (see Coates and Hillard 1986, pp.267–88). But in the 1950s that, too, lay unseen beyond the horizon, as British industry enjoyed its last sustained period of expanding employment and production.

> From 1951 to 1966 output of manufacturing grew 3.2% per annum on average, and then at 3% per annum 1964–73. The amount of capital going into industry was a record average for Britain of 3.3% per annum; employment in manufacturing increased by an average 0.2% per annum from 1951 to 1964 (1965–6 was the peak year in absolute numbers employed in manufacturing); then began a decline of 1.6% per annum 1964–73. As these figures suggest, total factor productivity in manufacturing improved by 2% per annum 1951–64, and by 3.1% per annum 1964–73.   (Ackrill 1987, p.184)

Industrial relations in Britain knew a period of immense calm not simply because Keynesianism dominated the thinking of successive Chancellors of the Exchequer, but because Late Capitalism was enjoying 25 years of unprecedented economic growth under the American dollar empire.

III

So long as the boom lasted, and so long as the competitive weakness of British industrial capital remained obscure, industrial relations did not figure as a major issue in national political life in Britain. For under those conditions, the State stayed out of industrial relations: holding the ring with a set of property and labour laws, but not actively pursuing any industrial relations reform. The easy competitive conditions experienced by British-based industry in the early years of the boom left the State free, as an employer, to pursue policies of wage increases and employment expansion that brought it into no major confrontation with its own workers; and for similar reasons workers were able to put aside any necessity to link their concerns as wage bargainers within the factory and the office with any wider involvement by them in the labour movement and its politics. Some workers were still politically active, of course; but the powerful imperative to be so that had been imposed between the wars by mass unemployment and state indifference seemed for a while to be a thing of the past.

What full employment did was to transform relationships of power within industry—and to do so in so fundamental a way that it touched every aspect of industrial life. As John Goldthorpe observed in an article written when unemployment was still low:

> Because of the improved market situation of industrial workers, because of their more effective organisation at shop floor level, their greater self-confidence and heightened wants and expectations, management has become less able than before to, as it were, fill in the 'silences' in the employment contract to its own advantage. Workers can now often prevent management from using its power in an entirely arbitrary or summary fashion; they can compel managements to negotiate and bargain with them on a widening range of issues; and, in these and other ways, they are able to call into question managerial 'prerogatives' the exercise of which in the past must be seen . . . as the expression of a superior power position.   (Goldthorpe 1974, pp.193–4)

Under these conditions, co-operation rather than coercion became the order of the day, and significantly placed groups of workers found that they could engage in a sort of 'do it yourself reformism'—could steadily improve their own living standards, enhance their own job control, and guarantee their own security of employment, without having to rely on outsiders: on national trade union leaders, on Labour politicians, or on a benign government. This shift in class power was well understood by contemporary commentators and political figures. Tony Crosland, for example, spelt out its ramifications clearly as early as 1956:

> 'There has been a decisive movement of power within industry itself from management to labour. This is mainly a consequence of the seller's market for labour created by full employment.
>
> The relative strength of workers and employers does not, of course, depend solely on conditions in the labour market. It depends also on the political balance, the social climate, the degree of organisation of the two sides, and current views about the relation between wages on the one hand, and profits, employment, or the foreign balance, on the other. These factors had all changed in a manner favourable to labour even before 1939. Yet the strength of the unions was still severely limited by large-scale unemployment; and they were obviously, and knew it, the weaker of the two contenders.
>
> The change from a buyer's to a seller's market for labour, however, by transposing at once the interests, and therefore the attitudes, of the two sides, has dramatically altered the balance of power at every level of labour relations.
>
> At the level of the individual worker, the decisive change relates to the question of dismissal. The employee, for whom dismissal before the war was often a sentence of long-term unemployment, can now quickly find a job elsewhere; and he has lost, in consequence, his fear of the sack, and with it his docility. The employer, on the other hand, who before the war could replace a dismissed worker from a long waiting list of applicants for jobs, may now have difficulty in finding any replacement at all; and he has acquired, in consequence, a reluctance to dismiss, and himself has become more docile. Thus the balance of advantage is reversed, and the result is a transformation of relationships at the shop-floor level.
>
> At the level of the plant or firm, the main change lies in the altered attitude of the two sides towards their ultimate weapon of coercion—the strike and the lock-out. With unemployment, the employer can often well afford to endure a strike or initiate a lock-out; the odds in the contest are on his side, while the cost of a stoppage, with stocks often high and market conditions unprofitable, may be relatively minor. But with full employment, the odds are quite different, since the workers can now hold out much longer; while the cost of a stoppage in terms of profits foregone is likely, with stocks perhaps low and a lucrative market demand, to be much greater. The employers' incentive to avoid strikes has thus increased in the same measure as the workers' prospects for winning them; the implications for the balance of power are obvious.
>
> (Crosland, cited in K. Coates 1982, pp.175–6)

Not all workers, of course, experienced such a massive transformation in their relationships with their employers. Instead, these shifts in class power were most heavily concentrated in the new growth industries of vehicle assembly, chemicals and light engineering. For these were the industries in which skilled labour was particularly scarce, and in which the sales departments experienced little foreign competition. As a result, these were the industries which were well-placed to pass on wage rises and associated costs to consumers in the form of higher prices. They were also industries which were highly capitalised, in which labour productivity was high and labour costs only a small percentage of total outlay; and so they were industries in which the incentive to avoid strikes (to keep capital fully operative) was high while that to keep wages down was commensurately weak. And they were industries too in which constant product differentiation necessitated regular changes in work specifications and terms of employment, and in which systems of payment-by-results gave immense scope to local bargaining. These were the industries in which the Donovan Commission found by 1968 the existence of a well-entrenched 'second' tier of industrial relations beneath the national bargaining systems to which the industries formally subscribed.

Industrial relations in the engineering industry in particular were characterised by this two-tier system. At national level, company representatives and full-time trade union officials nego-tiated national minimum wages and conditions of employment. But these were supplemented locally by a 'largely informal, largely fragmented and largely autonomous' system of local bargaining between companies and shop stewards representing well-organised and self-confident work groups. This system was 'informal because of the predominance of unwritten understand-ings and of custom and practice. It was fragmented because it involved individual shop stewards or relatively small groups of workers. It was autonomous because it rarely involved the employers' organisation or trade union officials and had little or no relationship with the terms and conditions of the multi-employer agreement' (Sisson and Brown 1983, pp.138–9). Work groups, shop stewards and full employment went together, as early commentators were quick to grasp. Arthur Marsh argued, for example, that:

> If the role of the steward can only be explained, at bottom, in terms of the work group, his effectiveness in that role and more recently his rapid rise in authority over the economy as a whole can only be explained in terms of general labour scarcity. Until recently, the

work group has only in exceptional circumstances been able to
apply its working rules to the workplace so as to make its bargaining
position felt by management.

(Marsh, cited in Goodman and Whittingham 1969, p.72)

As that situation changed in the late 1950s, as prolonged
full employment strengthened working class self-confidence and
assertiveness, the number and activities of shop stewards became
of increasing concern to commentators and politicians alike.
Estimates of the number of shop stewards varied widely. Clegg,
Killick and Adams guessed at 90,000 in 1961, Marsh and Coker
suggested anything between 100–120,000 in the early 1960s, and
the TUC annual report in 1960 thought the number might be as
high as 200,000. But there was no disagreement on the fact that
'the number of stewards had increased since the war. After
examining AEU records, Marsh and Coker suggested that the
increase was about 50% between 1947 and 1961 . . . and (that)
the number of AEU shop stewards in federated establishments
increased three times faster than that of manual workers in such
establishments in 1947–61' (ibid., pp.38–9).

Nor was there much disagreement on what stewards did. As
the later Lord McCarthy told the Donovan Commission, they
negotiated 'over a wide range of issues, from the level of piecework earnings to non-financial questions such as discipline and
conditions of work' (McCarthy 1966, p.16). At much the same
time as Donovan gathered his evidence, Shirley Lerner found shop
stewards in engineering plants in five cities negotiating on trade
union and shop steward status, hours of work, redundancy, work
rules, personnel records, and other miscellaneous provisions
(see Goodman and Whittingham 1969, p.162). By 'withdrawal of
forms of co-operation', insisting on 'formal rights and customs',
creating 'output limitations and restrictions on hours of work' and
organising 'withdrawals of labour' (McCarthy 1966, p.19), shop
stewards by the early 1960s were effectively obliging managements
to consult and negotiate on a large percentage of the immediate
rules and agreements covering the use, number, work pace and
job security of manual workers in engineering, in chemicals, and in
printing.

This 'challenge from below', as apologists for managerial power
called it at the time (Flanders 1970, p.108), was patchy in its
coverage and impact. Not all stewards negotiated on all issues. Not

all work groups had the same power to exploit the negotiations into which their stewards entered; and local managements varied, both between firms and within the same firm over time, in the degree of job control they were prepared to surrender to the work groups and stewards that they faced. Yet the majority of personnel managers from large private multi-plant firms surveyed for the Donovan Commission in 1968 actually preferred dealing with shop stewards to dealing with full-time trade union officers, because of the former's 'intimate knowledge of the circumstances of the case'; and the researchers found that real opposition and resentment to shop stewards among senior managers was 'confined to a small minority' (McCarthy 1966, pp. 66 and 67). By then, labour shortages, easier product market conditions, and highly capitalised production systems had long obliged them all to make some surrender of their authority to stewards and work groups. Indeed, 'managements had, according to the Donovan Commission, lost much of their control over the detail of work arrangements to fragmented work groups; earnings, particularly where piecework operated, "drifted" upwards, yet few employers seemed seriously concerned at this state of affairs' (Hyman 1973, p.111). For to the degree that this was so, managers in British industry had also come in the process to tolerate a more even distribution of power within British industry between capital and labour than had ever been seen before.

The result was a situation which, in the late 1960s, was summarised by Goodman and Whittingham (1969) in this way:

> With full employment and buoyant product markets, work-groups have enhanced their influence, largely through the agency of shop stewards. Management styles have, by design or necessity, come to be more consultative than the old autocratic methods. Labour scarcity, expensive training, rapid technical change, and the teachings of human relations doctrines have emphasised the desirability of this style. In the last resort, the added impact of sanctions available to employees has induced management to lead rather than drive, the consent of organised employees being necessary to continued operations. In large plants, obtaining consent demands a representational system, and thus places the occupants of this representative role in a strategic position. With the support of their members, shop stewards can determine the terms and conditions of consent. These developments have enabled shop stewards to emerge as a semi-independent force in the industrial relations system, with tenuous ties with the old

established machinery. They have achieved bargaining functions on a multitude of directly and indirectly pecuniary topics, and on issues concerned with workers' status and rights, which cumulatively have a powerful influence on the total working environment. This change, unevenly consolidated within British industry, partly reflects and is partly a cause of the changing power structure within and beyond the workplace.   (pp.7–8)

The national systems of multi-employer collective bargaining within which shop stewards operated had been put together at district levels towards the end of the nineteenth century, and consolidated at national level between the wars in the very different conditions of large-scale unemployment. Such agreements between the wars had left management totally free to act where the agreements were silent, blocked only by any vestigial craft controls or isolated pockets of industrial militants. The shop stewards movement which had flourished briefly in the favourable labour conditions of the First World War had not survived the unemployment and defeats of the 1919–26 period, and so was unavailable to challenge this inter-war exercise of unlimited managerial authority. Shop stewards only began to appear again as local bargainers when employment rose in vehicle manufacture with re-armament in the late 1930s. Then 'the spread of payments by results, the attack on craft controls by the "scientific management" movement, and the wholesale transformation in workshop practices during wartime, all stimulated the rapid growth of workplace collective bargaining, and the rise in the number and status of shop stewards' (Hyman 1975, p.152). During the war, motor manufacturers were eventually obliged by the Ministry of Labour to recognise trade unions, and by the pressure of labour shortages to negotiate with stewards; and those stewards, 'faced by managements which were typically unsophisticated, unco-ordinated and indecisive, were well-placed both to push up earnings and to exact a high degree of job control' (Hyman 1980, p.67).

Where managements were neither unsophisticated nor unco-ordinated, however, it took longer for stewards to break in. Unionisation at Morris Motors, for example, 'was a mere 25% in 1956, Vauxhall and Ford were under 50%: Austin's density was higher, but stewards' actions were restricted and ineffective' (Cronin 1984, p.180). It was only by the late 1950s that shop stewards in the motor vehicle industry, in engineering, printing, and the chemical industry became well entrenched, as work groups and their unofficial representatives re-asserted 'far beyond the original craft context . . . prior traditions of autonomous worker control' (Hyman 1975, p.158). To an extent without parallel elsewhere in the industrial relations systems and labour movements of advanced capitalism, the organisation of the labour process in the late 1950s and 1960s came to be characterised by the three features which—in their uniqueness—would later be singled out by a hostile press as constitutive of *the English disease*: restrictive practices, wage drift and unofficial strikes.

In these industries, strategically placed workers had already by the early 1960s won significant degrees of control over local bonuses, manning levels, job demarcation, overtime, and the pace of work. The gap between nationally negotiated wage rates and actual levels of earnings was already wide and growing, and outstripping levels of productivity growth in British industry as a whole; and in these industries, too, those powers were protected, when challenged, by short unofficial industrial disputes. The explosion of militancy in the late 1950s and early 1960s that accompanied the consolidation of shop steward power in the car industry is well captured in Table 2.3.

Table 2.3 Industrial Disputes in Car Firms, 1947–64
(annual averages of three-year periods)

	No of separate strikes	No of workers directly or indirectly involved	Days lost
1947–9	10	9,000	25,000
1950–2	14	25,000	131,000
1953–5	14	42,000	137,000
1956–8	31	82,000	322,000
1959–61	75	116,000	307,000
1962–4	86	141,000	321,000

Source: Friedman (1977) p.215.

Contemporaries were well aware of this 'great post-war challenge which had surged up from below', as Allan Flanders put it (1970, p.108); and they knew, too, that what was at stake here was much more than a simple question of wages, vital as these were. Industrial disputes in the late 1950s went far beyond a struggle over money and hours, as Professor Turner made clear in 1963 when he reported that:

> In the twenty years of high employment from 1940, the proportion of strikes about 'wage questions *other than* demands for increases', and (particularly) about 'working arrangements, rules and disciplines' rose remarkably: from one-third of all stoppages to three-quarters. Now a close look at disputes so classified suggests that their increases mainly involve three types of demand. First, for what some have called an 'Effort Bargain'—that is, for the amount of work to be done for a given wage to be as explicitly negotiable as the wage itself. Secondly, for changes in working arrangements, methods and the use of labour to be also subject to agreement—or to agreed rules. And thirdly, they concern the treatment of individuals or groups by managers and supervisors. One *could* say that these disputes all involve attempts to submit managerial discretion and authority to be agreed—or failing that, customary rules: alternatively, that they reflect an implicit pressure for more democracy and individual rights in industry. But on this trend, the last two or three years have superimposed another: a sharp rise in the frequency of unofficial strikes against dismissals and—at last— for wage increases. So far, in effect, from reducing the frequency of unofficial disputes, recent unemployment and economic stagnation have increased it by outraging *now*-established expectations— expectations of security and an automatic annual increase in income, such as salaried employees commonly enjoy.
>
> (cited in Flanders 1970, p.111)

In specifying that pattern of industrial disputes as politically significant in the 1950s, we must not, however, fall into the trap into which the British State itself can be said to have fallen in the decade after 1964, of over-generalising the 'challenge from below'. The challenge, as we have seen, built up in the core growth areas of British industrial capital in the late 1950s: in engineering and motor vehicle construction in particular, and in industries such as printing where work groups gathered considerable industrial 'muscle' because of the unique perishability of the commodity which they produced. There, 'shopfloor organisation and bargaining, relatively isolated from the constraints of national agreements and national trade union leadership' had 'facilitated the maintenance of a multiplicity of controls over the management's deployment and application of labour power', controls which were 'more extensive and more effective . . . than in most other countries' (Hyman and Elger 1981, p.118). But we must remember that 'a considerable contrast existed in much of the public sector, within most white collar occupations, and even among a wide range of private sector manual workers' (Hyman 1988, p.9) where work groups failed to establish any equivalent power. Certainly there was no 'challenge from below' by the majority of public sector employees in the 1950s. They did not generate any strong shop steward organisation. Nor did they, in the main, establish a wide gap between nationally-specified wage rates and actual earnings. Instead, they remained throughout the 1950s and 1960s heavily dependent on nationally-negotiated wage agreements where the criterion of 'comparability' with equivalent private sector wages, and the extensive use of arbitration machinery, did much to mitigate the tensions between employers and workers characteristic of wage negotiations in the private sector. Indeed, partly for this reason, government employees in the 1950s were rarely drawn into industrial disputes. Strikes were things that happened between private employers and workers in the main, and only occasionally extended to municipal bus companies or nationalised industries.

The mining industry alone stood as a significant exception. Miners remained the most strike-prone group in British industry until 1957, responsible for three quarters of recorded stoppages, most of which were 'small and short, and all (of which) up to 1972 (were) unofficial' (Hyman 1972, p.29). But even here militancy then waned, and the industry contracted rapidly without major resistance either from the NUM or from unofficial strikers. 'Up to 1958 the number of men employed in coalmining fluctuated around the 700,000 level, but then started a decline which continued until 1970–71, when it (briefly) settled at 287,200 as the annual average' (Hughes and Moore 1972, p.13). At the same time, the industry saw a 'dramatic decline' in the number of recorded stoppages: 'from 2,224 mining strikes in 1957 to 165 in 1970', as the number of striker-days in mining 'fell during the 1960s to the average of industry generally' (Hyman 1972, p.29). So it did seem, by the early 1960s, that major industrial disputes even in this traditionally militant part of the public sector were a thing of the past; and that the centre of gravity of industrial relations in

Britain had indeed shifted to the new workers in engineering and motor vehicle construction.

That shift, however, was more apparent than real. Indeed, from the early 1960s, when successive British governments began to address themselves to this 'challenge from below' in British manufacturing industry, they were eventually to see their initiatives blocked, not by resistance in the engineering and motor assembly industries, but by the renewed militancy of their own employees caught in the cross-fire. This resurgence of *public sector* militancy, generated by attempts to handle *private sector* working class power, will be a major concern of the next chapter; but few people had any inkling of its coming as the 1960s began. For then, unaware of upon how fragile a base the industrial relations consensus of the 1950s rested, commentators on that consensus were overwhelmingly preoccupied with the rise of workplace bargaining in the engineering heartlands of British industrial capital. What they saw impressed them with its 'maturity' and its 'sophistication'—and with what Otto Kahn-Freund, the leading academic lawyer writing in this field in the 1950s, called its 'subtle and civilised web of mutual obligations', its 'dynamism' and its 'flexibility' (cited in Fox 1985, p.370).

IV

The experience of this 'flexibility' in the late 1950s by workers in engineering and motor vehicle construction was to have profound and long-term consequences for the politics of industrial relations in Great Britain. The existence of shopfloor power, and the impact this had on rates of accumulation and levels of profit in British manufacturing industry, would—as we shall see in the next chapter—bring workers regularly into conflict with successive governments in the 1960s and 1970s. The fact that for eleven of the fifteen years after 1964 those governments were Labour ones would in the end seriously weaken the hold of the Labour Party on the voting loyalties and wider social and political attitudes of key groups of British workers. It would in that way play a critical part in the reconsolidation of Conservative domination of British politics under which we all currently operate. But the fact that the failure of Labour after 1964 eventually sent workers in Britain towards the Right—and not off in a search for some more genuinely socialist alternative to Labour's programme—is rooted further back. Its explanation lies in the way in which the 'easy' industrial relations conditions of the 1950s helped to *depoliticise* key sections of the British working class, and to consolidate in them highly *instrumental* attitudes to both Labour politicians and national trade union organisation.

The evidence of that 'depoliticisation' and 'instrumentality' was there in abundance in the findings of the much-quoted *Affluent Worker* studies carried out among Luton car workers in 1962. The study was a direct response to three successive defeats for the Labour Party in general elections (in 1951, 1955 and 1959), and to the explanation of that pattern of defeat then widespread on the Labour Right: namely, that the rising affluence of English workers was eroding their radicalism by fusing them into the middle class and into its associated Conservative style of life and politics. John Goldthorpe and David Lockwood's study clearly demonstrated the superficiality of that analysis of Labour's problems in the 1950s. The men they studied in Luton still had a very different set of work experiences and life styles from those common among the middle class with whom they were supposed increasingly both to fuse and to identify. To come anywhere close to the income of a lower professional, these car workers had to tolerate working conditions, degrees of supervision, an intensity of effort, and systematic overtime, that were the obverse of a typical professional working routine; and as 'affluent workers' they still experienced levels of job insecurity, and a pattern of earnings over their life cycle, which again were qualitatively different, and distinctly poorer, than those typical of many middle-class professions. Nor did the 'new' workers socialise with, identify with, or aspire to join, such occupational groups. On the contrary: they still saw themselves as members of the working class, operated with a 'them' and 'us' vision of social inequality, and were both trade union members and Labour voters. 'In Luton, purposely selected as a place likely to exhibit the new attitudes following upon affluence, class feelings . . . remained distinct and resistant. Manual and white collar workers seldom mixed, nor did their families: middle class styles of consumption, entertainment and aspiration remained the property of the white collar employees only, and not all of them: and working people kept to themselves and wanted it that way' (Cronin 1984, p.171).

The seeds of Labour's electoral decline could not therefore be found in any diminution of either the experience or consciousness of class divisions in Macmillan's Britain; and indeed the revival of Labour's electoral fortunes in 1964 and 1966 effectively silenced such a banal argument. But the brevity of that revival, and its cataclysmic collapse after 1970, could still be seen in embryo in the *quality* of the consciousness of class divisions that the Luton study—preoccupied with routing the arguments on affluence—inadvertently unearthed.

The Luton car workers in 1962 demonstrated all the classic signs of proletarian alienation. For them, work had no intrinsic rewards. Indeed, on the contrary, work was experienced as unsatisfying labour, undertaken purely for its monetary return. These men had 'in effect chosen to abandon employment which could give them some greater degree of intrinsic reward in favour of work which enabled them to achieve a higher degree of economic return' (Goldthorpe *et al.*, Vol.1, 1968, p.33); and as such they sought, not a career within the firm, but money from it, to justify the repeated sale of their labour power under dismal conditions. But this commitment to cash, and the alienating experience of labour, did not generate among these men any traditional solidarities of class, or any commitment to collective socialist advance. For they were 'privatised' workers, with family-centred and consumer-oriented aspirations, who did not even socialise extensively with the people with whom they worked. 'Most spent their spare time at home, in front of the television or in the garden, and combined their desire to acquire more goods with a wish to enjoy their possessions alone, or as part of the nuclear family (Cronin 1984, p.170). In place of the old working-class community of factory, hearth and pub, Goldthorpe *et al.* reported on the existence of a new privatised worker emerging in the relatively well-paid conditions of British manufacturing industry in the early 1960s.

Such 'privatised workers' were not hostile to collective institutions and action. 87% of them were trade union members. 83% voted regularly for their stewards, and 80% of them had voted Labour in 1959 (and intended to do so again in 1964). These men were stable and loyal trade unionists and Labour supporters. They were well aware that they could only achieve their individual and privatised goals through collective action with their fellow workers. But this realisation gave them only a highly instrumental and calculative attitude to the collective institutions made available to them by the labour movement. They joined unions, voted for stewards, and supported the Labour Party, for what those institutions could give them directly; and they were prepared to participate in local union affairs (they did not in either national trade union matters or even in the local Labour Party) only because of the local union's immediate pay-off to them through negotiations with local management. In fact, so instrumental in their attitudes to unionism were they, and so vulnerable to popular media hostility to trade unions, that 41% of them were already prepared to say—as early as 1962—that national trade unions had too much political power. There is just no overwhelming evidence in the Luton study that these men saw either trade unions or the Labour Party as part of any wider, radical, class-based movement. Instead, the Luton workers were highly instrumental in their attitude to collective action. Not for them the more solidaristic collectivism of a proletarian socialist struggle. As Goldthorpe and Lockwood found:

> In four out of the five occupational groups, a majority felt that unions should limit themselves to their specifically economic functions: only among the craftsmen was the idea of greater worker control still largely upheld as a union objective. . . . in the consciousness of many of our affluent workers, the political involvement of their union is not a matter of any great saliency; and . . . that of those who are most politically aware, a sizable number are not prepared to support their union in its affiliation to the Labour Party. In sum it is fairly clearly indicated that these workers are not to any large degree committed to the traditional idea of the trade unions and the Labour Party as forming the industrial and political wings of an integrated labour movement.
> (Goldthorpe and Lockwood, Vol.1, 1968, pp.108 and 111)

We must be clear on what had, and what had not, happened by 1962. What the authors of the Luton study suggested was not a *diminution* in support by these car workers for the Labour Party (that would come later) but a change in its *nature*. Goldthorpe and Lockwood were aware, as we must be, that they must not create an unsubstantiated image of some 'socialist golden age' in the past when workers had a wider vision. They recognised the lack of comparable evidence for earlier periods. They knew that wages and conditions of work always—and of necessity—were of prime concern to workers and their families. And they knew, too, that the image of a 'traditional worker'—one who had strong class loyalty, valued mutual aid and gregarious living, dwelling in a closed and highly integrated working-class community, and demonstrating, as they put it, 'solidaristic collectivism'—was just that: an image, an ideal type against which to throw the working class of 1962 into conceptual, not historical, relief. (On this, see Lockwood 1975, *passim*.) And yet the legacies of some past of that sort were still evident in the Luton findings. These workers still regarded 'the unions and the Labour Party as organisations which could have some special claim on their allegiance; and still saw the Labour Party as a class party' (Goldthorpe *et al.* 1968, p.80). But these older, received views of the Labour Party and class were now filtered through a highly instrumental and largely family-centred set of concerns, which left the Luton workers as 'habitual rather than enthusiastic' (Westergaard 1970, p.125) Labour supporters, with only 'a limited and conditional commitment to the established organisations of the labour movement' (ibid., p.126). It is worth quoting Goldthorpe *et al.* fully on this:

> Even if embourgeoisification is not occurring on any significant scale, it is still likely that within the working class the commitment to collective means of achieving economic goals—most notably, the commitment to trade unionism—is weakening, and likewise, support for 'labour' objectives, and for the Labour Party in national politics. . . . It is mistaken to suppose that the economic and social attitudes characteristic of (these new workers) . . . are incompatible with their continued adherence to the traditional *forms* of working class collectivism: that is, trade unionism and electoral support for the Labour Party. . . . However, although these groups may still regard the unions and the Labour Party as organisations which have some special claim on their allegiance, their attachment to them *could* certainly become of an increasingly instrumental—and thus conditional—kind, and one devoid of all sense of participation in a class *movement* seeking structural changes in society or even pursuing more limited aims through concerted class action.   (cited in Blackwell and Seabrook 1985, pp.105–6)

On attitudes to the Labour Party, Goldthorpe and Lockwood's findings were distinct and clear:

To be sure, the conception of the Labour Party as a 'class' party was very much in evidence in the replies given when our affluent workers were asked to account for their attachment to Labour. At the same time, though, in addition to these expressions of a diffuse sense of class loyalty, some of our men also took the view that the Labour Party commanded their allegiance because, by contrast with other parties, it is the one which can do most for the ordinary working man in the way of increasing living standards and improving the social services. And moreover when the workers who intended to vote Labour at the next General Election were considering the significance of a possible Labour victory, they saw this largely in terms of the economic pay-offs which might be expected from a Labour Government. The sober calculation of such material advantage is not, of course, incompatible with sentiments of class loyalty. But other evidence that we collected does suggest that our 'affluent workers' support for Labour is probably less solidaristic and more instrumental than that of the many traditional workers from whom the Labour Party has in the past received almost unconditional allegiance.

> (Goldthorpe *et al.*, Vol.2, 1968, pp.30–31)

Though the people surveyed in Luton cannot easily be taken as typical of the working class as a whole (they were in the main young semi-skilled males working in mass production industry), the broad conclusions reached from Goldthorpe and Lockwood's interviews with them were mirrored in a range of other studies carried out at much the same time. In W. Runciman's more general survey of 'Relative Deprivation and Social Justice' undertaken in 1966, the workers interviewed, like the Luton ones, chose very limited 'orbits of comparison' when asked about the adequacy of their incomes. A surprisingly large number of them thought they were well paid, and felt there were not many people paid appreciably better. 'Few workers compared themselves to managers, employers or well-paid professionals, and most seemed to have markedly working-class notions of a proper standard of living' (Cronin 1984, p.170). None of this, of course, stopped them engaging in industrial militancy. Indeed, such workers' attachment to money suggested (as was indeed to be the case) that strike action would be taken if rising living standards were blocked. Goldthorpe and Lockwood were even willing to concede that such a blocking of expectations might generate a renewed working-class interest in political radicalism (Vol.3, p.189). But the tenor of their initial findings suggested otherwise—that the social bases for political radicalism among manual workers were eroding: that 'a man who is able to gain a good deal for himself out of the existing system, will move towards a conservative and individualistic, rather than a radical and collectivist, outlook on economic and political issues' (Vol.3, p.165), and that 'instrumentalism' and 'privatisation' alike militate against commitment to collective organisation on any but a limited and discontinuous basis. Affluence may not rule out militancy; but it does erode active radicalism' (Westergaard 1970, p.115).

In fact, it was this pessimism about working-class support for any radical political project that brought the Luton study its sharpest criticisms, as a series of socialist writers re-emphasised the volatility of working-class attitudes and actions which alienation and the cash nexus necessarily created in an unstable capitalist world. Quite properly, Goldthorpe and Lockwood's socialist critics reasserted the capacity of radical political leadership to *relink* the private and instrumental concerns of the affluent working class to a political programme directed against capitalist control of wealth and the production process; and Goldthorpe and Lockwood themselves conceded much of this in their final volume, published in 1969.

The Luton study cannot therefore be taken as offering a timeless statement about the new working class. Instead, its findings must be used as one measure of how workers responded to a decade of full employment and rising living standards under a series of Conservative governments. In a decade in which governments were not directly and immediately involved in economic management at factory level, in which the contrast between the conditions of the 1930s and those of the present were lived and real ones for most people, and in which the Labour Party was in Opposition, full employment and rising if still low living standards had apparently combined to make politics in general, and Labour politics in particular, progressively irrelevant for key sections of British workers. The answers that Goldthorpe and Lockwood were given show that at least some sections of the British working class—'machinists and assemblers rather than craftsmen and other specialist workers' (Westergaard 1970, p.118)—went, after 1964, into an era of incomes policies and unemployment with their own attitudes to the Labour Party *already* highly instrumental and calculative: already possessing, that is, a *distance* on Labour politics, an indifference and a scepticism, that the years of Labour government were only to accentuate and deepen.

Of course, we must not exaggerate how much of the future decay of Labour Party–working class links was in place by 1962, nor must we miss the persistence of anti-capitalist elements in popular thought that a radical Labour Party might well have consolidated and developed. The Luton studies also show that 'although there had been a slight decline in the share of the working class vote going to Labour since the high levels of 1950–51, the link between Labour and its working class base, or conversely, between the workers and their political party, had persisted' (Cronin 1984, p.172). What all the surveys of the early 1960s suggest (and that includes the Luton one) was the *contradictory* nature of working class political attitudes in that period. After all, it was possible for Goldthorpe and Lockwood to emphasise instrumentality and privatisation, and to play down findings critical of the existing distribution of social power; yet others were equally able to point to the existence of 'a fair amount of evidence—from the Luton survey . . . other studies . . . and further recent work', to show that in the early 1960s 'social criticism co-existed with social apathy in British working class consciousness'; that elements of a counter-culture existed there 'critical in general terms of the established social order', 'individualistic aspirations . . . linked with a sense of social injustice and of the exploitation characteristic of an unequal power situation' (Westergaard 1970, pp.121, 124 and 125). Rising living standards did not take these elements of social criticism away. Affluence, by 1962, had not, as Cronin correctly argues, directly undermined 'the tie between the workers and their institutions'. Rather, it had transformed 'the manner and coherence of the linkage. Increased expectations . . . simply altered slightly the feelings workers had as they gave their loyalties to Labour or the unions, and perhaps elevated somewhat the standard against which working people judged the performance of each' (Cronin 1984, p.172). The sense of being working class remained fully intact in 1962. There was as yet no slippage on that from the figures recorded in the 1940s. But what was changing was the political *content* of that sense of class.

What the experience of 'affluence' in the 1950s had done was to drain away much of that limited Labourist content of working class political attitudes which had sustained Labour radicalism in the mid-1940s; and this then left the British working class vulnerable two decades later to a revitalised Conservative onslaught on Labourism* itself. Though the bulk of that Conservative revival had to wait until the 1970s, its seeds were laid before 1964; and it was the Labour Party's tragedy both to superintend this erosion of popular enthusiasm for its political projects during the years of affluence, and then to dissipate its renewed electoral mandate after 1964 to such a degree that the Conservatives could return to power—partly on working class votes—in 1979, and stay there ever since. The affluent workers who voted Labour into office in 1964 could not have anticipated how badly that party would serve them in power; and by the time they had learned that lesson, by 1979, significant percentages of them were just no longer prepared to vote Labour at all. The 'golden age' of British industrial relations began to unglue Labour's relationship with its proletarian base. The 'crisis' of British industrial relations, to which we now turn, then carried that separation one major stage further.

---

* LABOURISM is a term which will occur regularly in this text. It is meant to capture the dominant definitions of 'the political' enshrined in the political philosophy and practice of the Labour Party since 1900, and of its predecessor working class political organisations (mainly on the left wing of the Gladstonian Liberal Party). A 'Labourist' reading of working class political interests emphasises their discrete and limited nature, their attainability within capitalism, and their capacity for realisation through parliamentary channels. Labourism is to be contrasted, and saw itself as distinct from, and in competition with, both less radical and more revolutionary specifications of working class political interests: standing in opposition both to Conservative denials of any distinctly 'working class' political interests which required a separate working class party, and in opposition to revolutionary socialist arguments that working class political interests could only be realised by the total replacement of capitalism and its dominant classes. Keir Hardie defined Labourism at the founding conference of the Labour Party in 1900 as that body of political 'theory and practice which accepted the possibility of social change within the existing framework of society; which rejected the revolutionary violence and action implicit in Chartist ideas of physical force; and which increasingly recognised the working of political democracy of the parliamentary variety as the practical means of achieving its own aims and objectives' (cited in Saville 1973, p.215; see also Saville 1967, pp.43–72; Coates 1975, pp.5–8; and, for a wider discussion, Looker and Coates 1983, *passim*).

3

The Politicisation of Industrial Relations

The material basis of the 'golden age' of British industrial relations came to pieces in two broad stages, the first of which invited a 'corporatist' political response and the second eventually a 'monetarist' one*. The problems which dominated stage one— broadly from 1961 to 1973—were primarily British-based; those of the second stage, after 1973, were more international in origin and scope. Between 1961 and 1973 British politics became increasingly dominated by the emerging weakness of British industrial capital, and by the threat that emerging weakness posed to the full employment basis of the post-war settlement. After 1973 these problems were made worse, and to a degree overshadowed, by the collapse of American domination of the world capitalist bloc, and by the generalised crisis of Keynesian demand management to which that collapse eventually gave rise. The problems of industrial weakness in Britain were difficult enough to solve amid generalised international economic growth in the 1960s. They were significantly more difficult to handle later, when world

---

* The meaning of both terms is best explained by the detailed content of the two chapters which follow this one. For the moment, however, it is sufficient simply to take corporatism as a set of policies deriving from tripartite negotiations between representatives of capital, labour and the State; and monetarism as a different set of policies created in the absence of these negotiations.

economic growth was sluggish and erratic; and in both periods, governments in Britain found themselves obliged to turn their attention to, among other things, those patterns of class power in industry from which in the 1950s they had largely stayed away. The emerging crisis of British manufacturing industry, and the international instability of the world capitalist order after the collapse of the dollar and the Yom Kippur War, drew industrial relations back into the mainstream of British political life; and made questions of trade union power and working class resistance to managerial authority key items on the political agenda.

Both corporatism and monetarism constituted sustained political reactions to the emerging instability of the post-war settlement in Britain. As we have already seen, that settlement had rested on Keynesian policies which had themselves emerged from regular and close negotiations between politicians and peak organisations of capital and labour. As we will now see, the corporatist response took this tri-partism to its limits—going beyond a 1950s understanding of Keynesianism in pursuit of an effective 'social contract' on national industrial recovery that required a sharp break neither with full employment nor with the 1950s 'cult of equilibrium' between classes. Monetarism, on the other hand, then made that sharp break: rejecting Keynesian solutions to full employment and eschewing the cosy 'beer and sandwiches' relationship of Labour ministers and trade unionists. Governments pursuing a corporatist strategy sought to come to terms with union power, and to manage market forces to do so; while those adopting a monetarist approach preferred to come to terms with the market, and to manage the unions instead. But though the two strategies differed fundamentally in their specifications for government action, both involved major state-led transformations of industrial relations. So if, in the 1960s and 1970s, the diminishing competitiveness of British-based industry in a world of intensifying competition progressively transformed the *economic* context in which workers and managers negotiated terms and conditions of employment, corporatist and monetarist reactions to industrial decline then added to that by progressively altering the *political* context of those negotiations. In so doing they left the 1950s looking like a 'golden age' of industrial peace and full employment; one moreover to which, as yet, there has been no return.

I

The structural weakness of the British economy was hidden, for a decade after the war, by the industrial dislocation of the defeated Axis powers; and even when signs of industrial decay did begin to emerge, politicians and commentators were slow to recognise, and reluctant to concede, that the world role of the British State was no longer underpinned by an equivalent economic predominance. From as early as 1957 internal expansions of the economy sucked in imports that created balance of payments difficulties and jeopardised the international acceptability of sterling as a junior reserve currency to the dollar within the exchange rate system set up in 1944 at Bretton Woods. The fear of currency crises, the reluctance to devalue, and the unwillingness to cut back significantly on foreign military spending, left the Conservative Government after 1957 with no option but to depress internal levels of demand, and to initiate a cycle of 'stop go' internal economic expansions and contractions that further frustrated industrial investment and business confidence. By the late 1950s it was commonplace to concede that Britain was falling behind industrially, that costs here were disproportionately high, and that both investment and productivity were low by comparison to major industrial competitors. What Middlemas refers to as 'a sense of pessimism' (1983, p.8) began to spread through government circles as politicians, held in office by their ability to reproduce the terms of the post-war settlement (of full employment, basic welfare provision and rising living standards), found themselves progressively unable to do that; and so were drawn into the search for 'political' solutions to this emerging economic weakness. The politicisation of industrial relations in Britain in the 1960s and 1970s was to be one largely unintended consequence of that search.

The decline in the competitive position of industrial capital in Britain has been explained in many ways. Many features of contemporary or recent experience have been singled out by analysts of different political colours as particularly productive of decline. These range from trade union power through a defective education system, too adversarial a mode of politics, and too amateur a civil service, to failures of management, the lack of patriotism in private capital, and the disproportionate power of financial institutions in the lobbies of the State (see Coates and Hillard 1986, 1987, *passim*).

In fact, the politicisation of industrial relations occurred when governments tried to rectify economic weakness because beneath these surface causes lay intractable questions of class power. Industrial capital in Britain lost its competitive edge after 1890 because industrial interests proved too weak, within the coalition of dominant classes in control of the British State, at all the crucial moments of policy realignment. Whenever the exchange rate of the pound was to be fixed, or interest rates altered, or the question of state-led industrial restructuring posed, industrial requirements took second place to a coalition of financial interests keen to protect London's role as an international money centre and to a political class keen to maintain its own world role by foreign military spending and the protection of a strong currency. Then in the 1950s the competitive strength of industrial capital was weakened further by the new-found defensive industrial strength of a fully-employed labour force, and by the political concessions—on employment, taxation and welfare—won by this revitalised class in 1945. Not surprisingly, then, when governments felt the need to tackle diminishing competitiveness in the late 1950s, the question of class power began to assert itself. Governments were obliged either to attempt to harness the private power of capital and labour in a common task of industrial recovery—as would be the case with all the corporatist initiatives—or, when that failed, to challenge the distribution of class power at its weakest point, as with monetarism's assault on trade unions and full employment after 1979. In retrospect at least, the logic of government policy after 1957 was clear: faced with economic decline generated by the balance of class forces in contemporary Britain, governments tried first to harness that balance, and then, having failed to harness it, turned instead to break it.

But of course it was not seen in that way by politicians at the outset. Instead, and as usual, government policy edged its way tentatively forward, struggling both to comprehend what was happening and to resolve the contradictory set of class forces operating upon it. Surface appearances dominated initially.

Understanding of underlying blockages came only later. Indeed, the first response was less to analyse at home than to look overseas. For as Britain's industrial weakness became a political issue, the fact that 'others abroad' were seen as doing better inspired commentators to look for foreign models and to seek salvation in the adoption of foreign practices. By the late 1970s those models were American and Japanese, but in the late 1950s they were predominantly French. French 'planning' became the first canvassed solution to Britain's industrial decline as politicians were persuaded by their reading of French experience to strengthen the state over which they presided, and to expand its activities beyond the indirect management of a private economy into the creation of tripartite planning bodies within which to create and oversee nationally agreed economic goals.

The major institutional legatee of that French-inspired response was the National Economic Development Council (the NEDC/ 'Neddy') created by the Macmillan Government in 1962 as a forum within which government, capital and labour could sit, with equal formal representation, to discuss problems of mutual concern and to come to mutually-agreed national economic targets. As we shall see, this national forum was supplemented later, as economic difficulties deepened, by 'little Neddies', which sought to reproduce that common purpose at an individual industry level; and alongside the NEDCs, successive governments until 1979 periodically and in addition created blue-prints ('National Plans'), policies (particularly on incomes) and further institutions (Prices and Incomes Boards, Industrial Reorganisation Corporations, National Enterprise Boards), all of which were designed to increase the potency of the State as an agent of industrial recovery. The cumulative effect of all this was to create in Britain the embryo of a corporatist* state, one which even in its embryonic form could

---

* This is an appropriate moment to define this term with greater precision. There is now a vast literature on corporatism, within which the term has either a broad or a narrow meaning. Defined broadly, corporatism is normally understood as 'a system of interest representation in which the constituent units are organised into a limited number of singular, compulsory, non-competitive, hierarchically-ordered and functionally differentiated categories, recognised or licensed (if not created) by the state, and guaranteed a deliberate representational monopoly within their respective categories in exchange for observing

no longer ignore the procedures and outcome of what in the 1950s had come to be largely private negotiations in the area of industrial relations between managers and managed.

Once more caution is required, so that we neither exaggerate the novelty of what was done in Britain after 1962 nor overstate the depth of the changes involved. For many centuries, of course, the dominant form of representation tolerated by the British State has been a parliamentary one; and indeed in 1962 the long struggle fully to democratise these representative arrangements had only been recently completed (with the achievement of full adult suffrage in 1929). So no British government in 1962 was contemplating any fundamental break with parliamentary modes of interest representation. All that happened in the 1960s was that parliamentary structures began once more to be supplemented by new and non-electorally based representative institutions, and that these new corporatist bodies came to play a critical role in the settlement of economic policy and in the overseeing of industrial relations.

It is possible to say 'once more' here because non-electorally based modes of representation also have a long history. The very capitalist forces and processes which eventually obliged ruling groups in Britain to concede full parliamentary democracy also long precipitated within the British State a penchant for less public and more direct functionally-based systems of interest group access to political decision making. Prior to 1914 such direct access to key state officials had been almost entirely restricted to a privileged group of capital owners, and had occurred almost exclusively through a network of private social connections made and regularly renewed in English country houses and London clubs. But, as working class industrial and political power grew

---

certain controls on their selection of leaders and articulation of demands and supports' (Schmitter 1974, pp.93–4). More narrowly, corporatism is best understood as a 'political structure within advanced capitalism which integrates organised socio-economic producer groups through a system of representation and co-operative mutual interaction at the leadership level, and mobilisation and social control at the mass level' (Panitch 1986, p.136). It is this narrow definition of the term which is being used here; and the emphasis on 'embryonic corporatism' is meant to signal how limited a move even towards the narrow definition was involved in the 'tri-partism' of the Labour Government between 1964 and 1979.

after 1900, this social 'Establishment' had been reluctantly obliged to grant entry to government departments to the leaders of organised labour; and indeed at key moments of class struggle (especially between 1918 and 1926) the granting and use of such access had played an important role in blunting working class radicalism and in preserving capitalist power. So there was nothing new in 1962 in the Government granting privileged access to trade union leaders in return for their co-operation in consensus politics. What was significant about the creation of the NEDC was not that the unions were to be courted once more, but rather that by 1962 the need for a particular kind of consultation was seen as so vital by the Government that a new institution to handle it had to be called into existence.

In fact, we can best assess the significance of the government initiatives of the 1960s if we see them in the context of what in the previous chapter we referred to as 'the corporatist bias' in twentieth-century British politics, and if we examine more fully a feature of the post-war settlement to which we referred in passing then. For the problems posed for British governments by the existence of strong trade unionism, and by the perceived weakness of industrial capital, were not new in 1962. Both had occupied governments at different times before; and both had been handled then by the development of new channels of access to government for the key parties involved. The Ministry of Labour, for example, had been used since its creation as the instrument through which governments could 'reach' trade union leaders if they needed to; and throughout the 1930s ministries such as the Board of Trade had established close working relationships with senior figures in private industry, and with key companies in the sectors for which they had responsibility. Indeed, both these processes—of reaching out to the unions and of establishing close industrial links—went on apace under the exigencies of full war mobilisation after 1939, and in the first phase of the Attlee Government that followed: so that by the late 1940s, as we established in the last chapter, it was well understood throughout the British political system that both capital and labour (through their national representatives) could legitimately expect to be consulted regularly on both the general character and detailed application of government economic policy.

If anything, the decade after 1948 saw something of a 'retreat' by government departments from the close and detailed intervention in the economy which war and immediate post-war reconstruction had made essential; and as they retreated, some of the regular and close consultation of a tri-partite kind went into abeyance. But it was merely in abeyance—it lasted only for as long as governments were satisfied to engage in *indirect* economic management of a Keynesian kind. When politicians no longer saw this as enough, when their perception grew of the likely political costs to themselves of industrial decline, then the tradition of tri-partite co-operation was there to be re-activated. For 'long after planning controls had been abandoned in the late 1940s and early 1950s, politicians, managers, civil servants and trade unionists of that generation carried the memory forward, and tended naturally to revive it when internal and external problems a decade later began to impair their dream of permanently successful economic management' (Middlemas 1983, p.1). The most direct and immediate consequence of that re-activation was a greater degree of state involvement than hitherto in the settlement of the terms and conditions under which labour power was sold and utilised in contemporary Britain.

II

The literature on industrial relations uses the term 'voluntarism' to characterise the pattern of relationships between managers and managed which was to be put under challenge by state initiatives in the 1960s. The term 'voluntarism' was meant to capture primarily the absence of law—or more accurately, of lawyers, judges and courts—from the drawing up and enforcement of contracts of employment. There was a framework of law around industrial relations, of course, but it was just that—a framework—whose 'principal function (had) been to support at the margins a system of collective bargaining based primarily on the autonomy of the parties involved' (Hyman and Fryer 1974, p.195). As Otto Kahn-Freund put it:

> There is perhaps no major country in the world in which the law has played a less significant role in the shaping of these relations than in Great Britain and in which today the law and the legal profession have less to do with labour relations . . . British industrial relations

> have, in the main, developed by way of industrial autonomy.
> This notion of autonomy is fundamental and . . . it means that
> employers and employees have formulated their own codes of
> conduct and devised their own machinery for enforcing them.
>   (Cited in Clegg and Flanders 1954, p.44)

Unions tolerated such a system—indeed, largely preferred it—
because their experience of judicial review and state intervention
in the nineteenth century had been so unhappy. Employers this
century had had little cause to turn to the State for assistance
because, until the 1940s at least, they had been strong enough to
deal satisfactorily with their own workers unaided; and governments, as we saw in Chapter 2, felt no compulsion to intervene
directly in industrial affairs 'so long as the results of voluntary
collective bargaining posed no threat to their own policies'
(Hyman and Fryer 1974, p.196). When they did, as in the General
Strike, the State acted: but the period immediately prior to the
General Strike was the exception, not the rule; and both before
then, and after, state involvement in industrial relations was rare
and limited.

By the late 1950s, however, politicians and commentators were
becoming increasingly aware of three features of contemporary
industrial relations practice that reflected the rising power of
work groups in manufacturing industry and whose significance was
heightened—for the politicians at least—by their growing concern
with economic performance. The first of these features of
contemporary industrial relations to which commentators were
increasingly drawing attention was the incidence of *wage drift* in
manufacturing—the opening up of a gap between earnings and
nationally-agreed wage rates which caused the living standards of
workers to rise faster than the rate of growth of industrial
productivity. These earnings were seen to be running ahead of
wage rates and productivity because of the ability of work groups
to use local shortages of skilled labour to win local bonuses,
control over systematic overtime, and favourable piece rates. The
second feature of contemporary industrial relations, viewed with
increasing alarm by Conservative politicians, was the incidence of
unofficial strikes, 'the increase, from the later 1950s onwards in the
frequency of unofficial and unconstitutional strikes in all major
industries except mining' (Goldthorpe 1974, p.184). Politicians
were becoming increasingly aware of the way in which work

groups in manufacturing industry won their local power by acting outside officially-agreed procedures, and by by-passing (or rather short-cutting) trade union officialdom to strike locally, quickly and briefly, in the settlement of local grievances and bonuses in direct negotiations with local management. Finally, the media began to emphasise too the existence of what they termed *restrictive practices*, making politicians and their electorate conscious of 'the relative inefficiency in labour utilisation in British industry, traceable in some important part to over-manning, rigid job demarcation, the systematic control of output and other forms of work regulation upheld by groups of rank-and-file employees with, or more often without, the official support of their unions' (ibid., p.184). In fact, as we saw in the last chapter, few workers achieved anything like the degree of control in these matters enjoyed by professional bodies (of lawyers, accountants, and the like). But what was 'professional self-government' for the middle classes was redefined as 'restrictive practices' when pursued by the lower orders, as a groundswell of media-orchestrated public concern arose over what was collectively termed 'the English disease', and as the radical shop steward and the idle worker were created as objects of ridicule and concern in films like *I'm All Right, Jack* and *The Angry Silence*. The tone of the times is well captured in this extract from the 1961 OEEC survey, *The Problem of Rising Prices*:

> On the strength of its record to date the United Kingdom must be judged to have failed to respond satisfactorily to the new problems posed by full employment. . . . given the antiquated nature of the institutional arrangements in a number of industries, the weakness of central bodies on both sides, the lack of any clearly-defined norm for arbitrators to take as a guide when making awards, there can be no assurance that wage increases in future will be kept in line with the growth potential of the economy.
>
> (Cited in K. Coates 1982, p.176)

In fact, as this concern grew in official circles, two conflicting readings of what was going on, and of what action was required, began to emerge: one explicitly Conservative and the other more properly liberal. The Tory view would rumble under the surface of British politics for at least two decades after its first explicit formulation in 1958, bubbling into view occasionally but only coming fully into its own after 1979. Until then more liberal views held sway—views equally uneasy with working class industrial power, but less willing than Tory ones to turn to law for their resolution. The view 'which may perhaps be best labelled as "Tory" [was] the relatively simple and straightforward one that all three problems reflect[ed] the greatly increased, and now excessive, power of organised labour in a society committed to high levels of employment and social security' (Goldthorpe 1974, p.185). The most easily available form of that argument was the often-cited pamphlet, published in 1958, by the Inns of Court Conservative and Unionist Society, *A Giant's Strength*, which focused attention on what the right-wing lawyers (including the young Sir Geoffrey Howe*) saw as the privileged legal position of trade unions. Trade unions, we were told, enjoyed rights to break contracts without vulnerability to civil damages because of the 1906 Trades Dispute Act; and because they did, the ability to manage industry properly was being lost. Only mass unemployment had prevented the misuse of this privilege hitherto; and now, with full employment, the deleterious effect of the unions' special legal position was there for all to see. The Tory Right (and certain employers' organisations too) wanted a new Trade Union Act and tougher penalties for strikers; and they kept asking for these as economic crisis followed economic crisis in the Britain of the 1960s.

Their views were initially drowned, however, by an academic orthodoxy in industrial relations—the so-called 'Oxford School' led by Allan Flanders and Hugh Clegg—which was carried into public prominence by Hugh Clegg's central role in the drafting of the final report of the Donovan Commission on Industrial Relations published in 1968. In the Oxford view, wage drift, unofficial strikes and 'restrictive practices' arose not from the excessive legal privileges of trade unionism, but from deficiencies in the institutions of collective bargaining, which had themselves arisen because negotiating machinery had not kept pace with the new conditions of full employment and rising expectations. For these, as we saw in the last chapter, 'had had the effect of greatly increasing the significance of collective bargaining conducted at the level of the industrial enterprise, plant or workshop'

---

* Initially Chancellor of the Exchequer, and later Foreign Secretary, in Margaret Thatcher's Conservative Governments after 1979.

(Goldthorpe 1974, pp.186–7) far removed from the control and specification of national wage negotiators. As we saw then, 'two systems of industrial relations' had emerged, unco-ordinated and often in conflict the one with the other: one a nationally-specified set of wage rates emerging from agreed and codified negotiating procedures, the other a set of workplace negotiations free of formal procedural guidelines, based on custom and practice, and giving rise to agreements that were mostly tacit, or at least 'rarely set down in a systematic written form' (ibid., p.187). In these workplace negotiations, neither national management nor official trade unions were regularly involved, and through them even local management had lost control of key aspects of work organisation to work groups and their stewards.

To the Oxford school, this was 'anomie', an affront to industrial order. To the Donovan Commission it was, more prosaically, a 'loss of authority' by both management and unions in the workplace: a loss which *both* had an interest in correcting, via a *joint* campaign to re-establish control over shop stewards and their activity, through the negotiation of detailed, written and signed plant agreements. In general, the Donovan Commission advocated 'an intensification of the attempt' to incorporate trade unionism by 'the elaboration within the workplace' of 'those pressures which had traditionally proved successful at the level of national union leadership' (Hyman 1973, p.114). It recommended the formalisation of the shop steward's role inside the factory, the 'substitution of joint regulation' for areas of control exercised 'autonomously by workers . . . a greater involvement of trade union officials (in conjunction with higher management) in supervising industrial relations at the point of production; and the close integration of shop stewards within the official structures of trade unionism' (ibid., p.114). The thinking which underlined the Donovan approach is well captured in this extended extract from the critical essay by John Goldthorpe:

> To achieve this aim it is . . . necessary for management and unions to accept, first of all, that the problem of the loss of authority in the workplace is one which they have in common; and secondly, that the only way in which they can overcome it is by committing themselves to the idea that the regulation of both work and payment systems within their enterprise should be their *joint* undertaking. From the side of management this would mean

abandoning strict adherence to doctrines of employers' 'reserved rights' or of managerial 'prerogatives', and acknowledging the right of unions to seek to exert influences in all areas of decision-making . . . From the side of labour, it would correspondingly need to be conceded that under a system of joint regulation practices with no more than a 'customary' basis or ones established by unilateral shop floor action could be properly called into question: and that in appraising work and payments systems generally, technical rationality and cost effectiveness must become dominant criteria . . . Thus effective reform must mean a programme of far-reaching institutional reconstruction, of a kind which will have to be accomplished primarily by management and unions themselves: the role of the law should be restricted, as it has traditionally been in British industrial relations, to providing a helpful framework within which 'voluntary' action by the parties directly concerned may proceed.   (Goldthorpe 1974, pp.185 and 189)

What the Donovan Commission proposed, therefore, was a joint management–union campaign to reduce the autonomy of work groups and their stewards, a campaign supported at the margin by the State.* Donovan afforded no major role to the State, assuming that the 'anarchy' to which his report drew attention was generally unpopular, and that to emphasise it through extensive publicity would be enough to trigger 'voluntary' action by managements and unions to rectify it. The role of the State was to be largely restricted to the creation of a *Commission on Industrial Relations*, to encourage the proper implementation of plant-wide bargaining, and to encourage the drawing up of comprehensive written domestic arrangements between company managers and elected representatives of their workforce; and indeed Allan Flanders left Oxford to join that Commission when it was created in 1969. But exhortation was never likely to be enough

---

* It is not possible to discuss the politics of the Oxford school in detail. Yet it is clear that its key figures were heavily committed to a strengthening of trade unionism within a philosophy that attached importance to discipline, order and control in industrial relations. Allan Flanders himself was a fascinating figure active in Revisionist circles in the Labour Party in the 1950s. He was convinced that the Commission on Industrial Relations would benefit ordinary rank and file trade unionists; and he was prepared to use the Commission later, when one of the Commissioners, to strengthen collective bargaining rights for hitherto under-powered groups of workers. (For a sympathetic treatment of the CIR, and of the Donovan proposals, see Palmer (1986). For a more critical view, see Gabriel, 1978.)

to overcome inertia here. For managements and unions seemed disproportionately satisfied with the existing set of arrangements, so obliging the Commission to concede that they must have 'some important advantages which impress themselves upon the participants' (ibid., p.208); and governments were too pressed by immediate concerns to find the pace of any voluntary-led reform entirely satisfactory. So while largely anticipating and accepting the argument of the Donovan Commission that the 'challenge from below' was the challenge that had to be removed, governments went far beyond the Commission's recommendations in the search for its solution.

In fact, by the time the Commission reported, governments were already heavily involved in the campaign to shift class power in industry, and were already generating more legislative initiatives than Donovan had proposed. In particular, and from as early as 1961, successive governments had first attempted to slow the rate of growth of earnings by specifying wage norms beyond which settlements were not to be made. These *incomes policies* involved initially nothing more than the setting of voluntary targets, without legal underpinnings, targets which were applied rigorously in the public sector as an example to the private. There was a whole spate of these targets in the 1960s: a total pay pause in July 1961; a 'guiding light' norm of 2–2½% in 1962; a norm in April 1965 of 3½%; by July 1966, a six-months' 'freeze' on all incomes; 'a period of severe restraint' with a nil norm from January to July 1967; and wage norms of 3½% and later 4½% between July 1967 and the Labour Government's electoral defeat in 1970. The formulation of these wage norms totally transformed the context of collective bargaining in Britain. Wage negotiators, who in the 1950s had acted alone and in private, now had to organise their private negotiations conscious first of all of the relationship of what they did to what the government required. With the arrival of incomes policy industrial relations were, so to speak, politicised at a stroke.

But though politicised by the arrival of incomes policies, wage negotiations were not thereby subjected to effective political control. On the contrary: the incomes policies of the 1960s in the end proved insufficient to the task they set themselves, and were eventually defeated by two quite predictable and, as far as ministers were concerned, undesirable effects. Their disparity of treatment between sectors—with norms more rigorously applied in the public sector than in a private one still short of skilled labour—stimulated first resentment, and later industrial militancy, among the government's own employees, costing governments votes in key by-elections, and eventually bringing industrially-disruptive and electorally-unpopular 'winters of discontent'. In addition, the specification of wage norms got nowhere near the *causes* of wage drift. Such specifications focused only on the *effects* (and not on the underlying origins) of the well-entrenched industrial power of work groups and their stewards. In practice, therefore, these norms were effective only over the industrially weak, and failed to stop wage drift in those industries in which drift was most concentrated and where it was most damaging to the international trade position and profit margins of British capitalism. As a result, governments found themselves paying a heavy electoral price for policies which did not significantly shift the balance of class forces in industry as they required. Indeed, even as a mechanism merely for restricting the growth rate of wages, incomes policies turned out to be unimpressive in the long run. Before July 1966 they hardly affected the levels of pay outside the public sector at all, and their success between July 1966 and June 1967 (in reducing the increase in the total wage bill to 2%) was bought at the price of a growing wage explosion thereafter. Seasonally adjusted earnings rose by 8.8% between July 1967 and March 1968, by 7.6% in the next nine-month period, by 8.3% in 1969, and by 13.6 between January and June 1970 (on this, see Coates 1975, pp.122–3).

Incomes policies failed to shift class power (in engineering in particular) because they focused on nationally-negotiated wage rates and left unaffected local negotiations and the shop floor power of organised work groups. It was through the recognition of this, and because of the rapid realisation in government circles that local earnings ran ahead of wage rates and productivity because of the control enjoyed by shop stewards and work groups over levels of manning, job demarcation, work rates and overtime, that there quickly followed an important change in policy: the supplementation of incomes policy norms with the 'buying out' of these controls—or, as the Labour Governments of the 1960s preferred to put it, the 'removal of restrictive practices' by allowing pay settlements beyond the norm only in return for perceived changes in working practices that would enhance industrial productivity.

The recognition of this requirement pre-dated the arrival of Labour in office in 1964, and was in place before the Labour Government created the National Board for Prices and Incomes to superintend its incomes policies. The Conservative White Paper of 1962, 'Incomes Policy: the Next Step', had talked of exceptions above the wage norm as part of agreements with productivity clauses. But in 1962 this was little more than exhortation; and it was only after the 'freeze' of July 1966 that *productivity bargaining* began to spread rapidly across British industry. After that date the only wage settlements formally allowed through the Government's vetting system were those below the specified norm, or those with genuine productivity clauses within them. Indeed, by the late 1960s productivity concessions had to be made to justify even a settlement at or below the specified income norm. When the National Board for Prices and Incomes looked for productivity bargains to analyse in 1966, it could only find seven major ones; but by 1969 productivity agreements had been signed on behalf of over six million workers in a vast range of privately-owned industries, productivity agreements that involved the buying out of control of aspects of the job by management from shop stewards and organised work groups.

By the end of 1969, the six million-plus workers covered by productivity bargaining had made arrangements that met the Prices and Incomes Board's specification of what a Productivity Agreement had to involve: namely co-operation in any or all of 'reductions in overtime, the freer exchange of tasks between different groups of workers, the removal of restrictions on output, manpower reduction, and changes in patterns of work' (Clegg, in Flanders 1969, p.353). By 1969, to be allowed a wage rise, workers had to tolerate the more flexible use of their labour, had to accept rationalisations of their wage structures and work-study evaluation of their jobs, be prepared to accept more shift-working, the greater interchangeability of tasks and changes in their working practices, or enhanced managerial control over overtime. In other words, the very issues over which shop stewards had established some degree of control from the late 1950s (on piece rates, levels and flexibility of manning, overtime, and the rate and organisation of work) suddenly became the very changes that had to be conceded in order to win a wage settlement above the norm.

What was clearly happening was a state-led attempt to shift class power back to management across key sections of British industry. The fact that it was the Labour Party which was in government made no significant difference. On the contrary, the Labour Government's pre-occupation with the reduction in the power of organised work groups is clear in the way that managerial aims were adopted and publicised by Ministers and by the Prices and Incomes Board itself. The Board put its full weight behind the modification or buying out of piece-rate systems, and their replacement by tighter managerial specification of job content and times. Report 123 of the Board listed managerial aims in productivity bargaining, and gave them broad support: the increased flexibility in the use of manpower, the reduction of manpower, changes in working practices, the introduction of job evaluation schemes and changes in wage structure, and the establishment of managerial control of overtime (NBPI 1968, paras 11–13). In fact, the very way in which the Government's incomes vetting system and the NBPI worked—in close contact with local management but only loosely connected to even national trade union bureaucracies—allowed managerial perspectives, definitions and problems to dominate policy, and showed precisely with which side of the industrial divide the Government was allied.

As with incomes policy proper, however, the impact of state initiatives here varied with the degree of organisation and militancy of workers. Productivity bargaining undoubtedly hit the industrially weak, for to exploit productivity bargaining workers required a strong shop floor organisation, itself virtually a monopoly of the higher paid sections of the working class. Indeed, in its early stages (in 1967 and 1968) the policy was generally effective in holding down the movement in real wages, but thereafter its impact fell away. For many productivity deals turned out to be bogus, connived at by managements and shop stewards in situations of local labour scarcity. Many (especially among white-collar workers) actually strengthened shop floor organisation, by stimulating 'restrictive practices' which could be sold and shop stewards to sell them. And in any case, hostility to productivity bargaining grew on the shop floor as the resulting intensification of effort and the strengthening of managerial controls were experienced, and as the associated growth in unemployment (unemployment doubled between 1966 and 1969) undermined job security. As Jack Jones put it, 'the government got the productivity and the workers got the sack' (cited in Fels 1972, p.30): with a consequent and rapid lessening of working class enthusiasm both for productivity bargaining and for the Labour Government which advocated it.

By then, however, the ground of political debate had shifted once more, this time towards more direct legislation on trade union powers themselves. For the Donovan Commission, in spite of its general support for 'voluntarism' in industrial relations, had left certain hostages to fortune. One in particular was its proposal that trade unions should register with the Registrar of Friendly Societies if they were to enjoy the legal immunities of the 1906 Trade Disputes Act. By 1969 this question of *registration* had become crucial. For a government's capacity to specify the terms on which registration would be allowed opened the possibility of direct state control over both the *internal* organisational and *external* collective bargaining practices of trade unions. It also created the possibility that unions could be required to discipline their own militants in return for registration, and that judges could be left with the power to decide if the terms of registration were being met. Those signing the Majority Report to the Donovan Commission had only intended that the terms of registration should specify internal union procedures (on admission, elections, discipline and shop stewards); but by 1971 the Conservative Government was prepared to specify a list of 'external' requirements that the Registrar might be asked to impose—requirements that would eat away at the industrial potency of shop stewards by obliging the unions (if they wished to protect their registration) to police the behaviour of their own members in particular ways.

In going this far, the ground was prepared for the Heath Government by its predecessor's insistence on supplementing the Donovan proposals with additional legal powers to control certain kinds of strikes. The Labour Government's proposals here (in the 1969 White Paper, *In Place of Strife*) were relatively limited: that the Secretary of State for Employment should have the power to intervene in inter-union disputes, to order compulsory ballots before certain official strikes, and to require a 'cooling off' period in unconstitutional strikes (breaches of which would invite fines directly deductible from wages). These proposals, modest though they were in the light of what was to come after 1970, had two immediate consequences. They split the Labour movement down the middle, and they forced a Labour Government retreat (for details, see Jenkins 1970). Significantly, in that retreat, the Labour Government asked the TUC to discipline its own militants—even going 'so far as to propose to back up TUC rulings by state sanctions against strikers who refused to accept these rulings' (Panitch 1986, p.198). The TUC, of course, refused. The White Paper also put full-square on the political agenda the formulation of 'the strike problem' as articulated by the Conservatives and their allies in industry: namely that the trade unions were 'over-mighty subjects' whose power was in need of legal redress. As Barnes and Reid put it, 'the Labour Government (to the Conservatives' great surprise) had opened a door more or less closed in practical political discussion since 1927, and the Conservative Party could hardly walk away from it' (Barnes and Reid 1980, p.136).

So, in 1970, the Conservative Government proposed that collective agreements should be enforceable at law so long as at least one party to them (say the employer) wished to make them so. The Conservatives' Industrial Relations Act also created a new Industrial Relations Court to enforce those contracts, and to order cooling-off periods and compulsory strike ballots. In addition, the Act created a new Code of Industrial Relations Practice—one that banned unofficial and unconstitutional strikes, certain kinds of sympathy strike, strikes for a closed shop, and the blacking of goods; and the Act made trade unions responsible for the activity of their members under this Code, with registration (and therefore immunity from civil damages under the 1906 Act) available only to those unions which complied with these requirements. In effect, the 1971 Industrial Relations Act picked up suggestions in the Minority Report of the Donovan Commission, and ones canvassed in the Conservative Party's own 1968 pamphlet, *Fair Deal at Work*, that trade unions should be allowed to register only if they observed 'certain minimum standards of behaviour', conducting their 'industrial relations in such a way as not to hold back improvements in the standard of living of the community as a whole'. The Act then used that requirement to justify the outlawing of the main tactics used by shop stewards in the defence of their members' wages and job control, and to introduce a legal framework under which the official trade union structure became answerable for the unofficial actions of its members.

The Act created a situation in which unions refusing to register could be taxed heavily and lose their legal immunity in the courts. Under its terms, any breach of the Code of Industrial Relations Practice by individual trade union members would leave the unions legally responsible (obliged, that is, to pay 'compensation' to the employer at a level fixed by the new Industrial Relations Court) and with the individual trade unionists themselves open to civil damages. The Act also created a situation—later to be used to the Government's embarrassment by small anti-union employers—in which, in the middle of a dispute, an employer could go to the National Industrial Relations Court for a ruling banning industrial action of an unconstitutional kind—a ban which, if it was ignored, would leave strikers in contempt of court, open to fines and imprisonment. Thus, in the space of a decade, the 'two systems of industrial relations' that incomes policies had tried to 'exhort' into unity, and productivity bargaining had tried to 'buy' back together, were now to be 'ordered' together by the force of law, and by the threat of legal sanctions against both unions and their individual members if state directives were ignored.

It is also worth emphasising here that these legislative initiatives did not occur in a vacuum but were, in industry and in the wider society, part of a much more general assault on working class power. By the late 1960s British industrial capital was caught in a major profits squeeze, exposed by its own under-investment and out-moded industrial practices to the twin forces of intensifying international competition in its product markets and strong worker organisation in its factories. As a result, the larger industrial companies had already begun to pursue productivity bargaining before 1966; and in fact the Esso agreement made at its Fawley works in the early 1960s acted as a model and a spur in the formulation of the government's own guidelines on productivity bargaining. Throughout the 1960s, the more sophisticated employers continued to subvert shop steward power, not so much by direct assaults on shop stewards' rights but rather by expanding the shop steward's role and by incorporating stewards into more bureaucratised relationships with local personnel management. In fact, 'the 1971 Act reflected far more the anti-collectivist ideology of the Tory Right (and in particular an influential coterie of Tory lawyers) than the requirements of the dominant sections of British capital', where 'most large employers saw trade unions as useful adjuncts to the personnel function, rendering employee relations more predictable and allowing the consensual introduction of changes in work arrangements (most notably through the "productivity bargaining" then in vogue' (Hyman 1987, p.96).

Nonetheless, these more sophisticated voices were temporarily drowned—even in employers' circles in the 1960s—by more strident calls for legal curbs on union power. Certainly, the major employers' federations intensified the publicity and regularity of their demands for more legal curbs as the 1960s progressed, and they used the opportunity afforded by the Donovan Commission to press their case, influencing the Minority Report, and shaping the thinking of the Conservative Party. So, in the event, the Donovan Commission reported, and the Labour Government formulated the last stages of its incomes policy, amid a publicly-orchestrated campaign against the unions, whose content and intensity had no post-war precedent. By 1970 it was conventional in media and government circles to hold that the trade unions were too powerful and collective bargaining too anarchic; and that the decline in the competitiveness of British industrial capital was to be explained largely through the recognition of these two 'facts'. Trade unionism by 1970 faced a shrill media and an active employers' offensive as well as a steadily more hostile set of government policies.

III

Yet what we have to grasp, if we are to understand what followed, is that in spite of all that orchestrated anti-unionism, this series of attempts by both Labour and Conservative governments to shift class power away from workers actually *failed*—and was in fact seriously counterproductive. State initiatives in this period actually made the 'problem' to which they were addressed 'worse'. Government attempts to 'reform' industrial relations through incomes policies, productivity bargaining and new legislation may have been a spur over the long period to more 'voluntary reform' of collective bargaining by unions and employers acting privately together; but in the more immediate period they simply left workers stronger, better organised and more militant than they had been when the initiatives began. They did this by fuelling a pattern of resistance which, if initially sporadic, local and defensive, became by 1974 persistent, national and increasingly politicised. Incomes policies which began effectively, eventually collapsed with steadfast regularity. Productivity dealing lost its impact with similar speed; and legislative initiatives were no more successful. Amazing as it may seem from the vantage point of the late 1980s, the Conservative Government of the early 1970s just could not make its legislation stick. Instead, 'whenever the 1971 Act came into conflict with well-established institutions and practices, it was unsuccessful in obtaining compliance with its terms' (Engleman and Thomson, 1974, p.150). Indeed, far from being successful, this first systematic post-war attempt to shift class power from labour to capital actually ended with a level of industrial unrest in Britain on a scale, and with a range and political focus, unknown since the General Strike.

We should not find this resistance too surprising, for it merely drew attention to a very basic flaw in the whole Donovan approach to the reform of industrial relations. At the heart of the Donovan analysis lay the assumption that both sides of the industrial divide stood to gain by the greater formal specification of industrial relations practices, and that no one stood to lose. Now it is true that officialdom might in general stand to gain from the successful application of a Donovan-inspired strategy: both official management negotiators and official trade union representatives. But shop stewards and work groups would not benefit from such a formalisation. On the contrary, they would lose; and indeed the whole Donovan project was designed precisely to ensure that they would lose—lose power over wages, over working practices, over overtime, and over security of employment. The Donovan Commission treated the power of management over workers, and that of unions over their members, as similar in kind; and suggested that the creation of formal agreements at plant level would enhance both. But the interest of management in relation to workers was one of *control*, that of unions one of *representation*. Plant-wide agreements might add to managerial power but, if

implemented in the face of worker opposition, could do so only at
the cost of eroding the representativeness of trade unionism, and
of subordinating the union's capacity to represent its members to
an extra-union requirement to discipline them in the name of some
wider consensus. For as John Goldthorpe observed at the time,
the whole Donovan approach persistently ducked the question of
'how far one may regard the problems of either management or
union bureaucracies as being ones that are of great concern to the
men on the shop floor themselves'. If the 'problems' of wage drift,
unofficial strikes and 'restrictive practices' originated 'chiefly in a
shift of bargaining advantage towards the latter, why should it be
thought that they too will regard the existing state of affairs as in
evident need of reform?' (Goldthorpe 1974, p.195).

The Donovan approach to industrial relations was 'managerialist in its priorities and conservative in its implications'. The
changes it sought to implement were 'ones designed to bring about
the more effective integration of labour into the existing structure
of economic and social relations, in industry and the wider society,
rather than ones intended to produce any basic alteration in this
structure' (ibid., p.205). Restrictive practices, unofficial strikes
and wage drift were problems for governments seeking a competitive capitalism. They were problems for managers seeking to
regain control over all aspects of the work process. They might
even be problems for that section of the trade union bureaucracy
which accepted the dubious argument that Britain's industrial
decline was largely the result of working class power. But they
were certainly not problems for the work groups who benefited
from them; and as the unofficial power of those work groups was
attacked, workers engaged in an increasingly extensive and serious
unofficial struggle in their defence.

Resistance to the emerging attempt to curb wage drift, unofficial
strikes and working class job control was initially moderate and
constitutional. Public sector unions caught by Selwyn Lloyd's 1961
'pay pause' federated together in a white-collar equivalent to the
TUC called COPPSO—the Confederation of Professional and
Public Service Organisations—and sought representation in the
newly-created body of tripartite negotiation, the NEDC. When
this was refused—by a Conservative Government, one might
note, which guaranteed TUC monopoly of representation on the
NEDC in return for TUC participation—the major white-collar

unions slipped into the TUC one by one. The Local Government Officers' Union joined in 1964, and the main teachers' unions were all in by 1970. (See Volker 1966 and Coates 1972, *passim.*) The first formal response, that is, to incomes policy was the *uniting* of the entire labour movement under one umbrella organisation. Such, of course, is the way with corporatism.

The second response by workers to this pattern of state policy was to join trade unions in greater numbers. Far from breaking shop steward power, the offensive merely made obvious to more and more workers that they needed the protection of official trade union structures, since trade unions were visibly being drawn into important national negotiations, and since unofficial, local and spontaneous industrial action was under increasing challenge. Union membership rose dramatically in this period, as Table 3.1 shows; and stretched out to take in workers in industries traditionally difficult for the unions to reach.

Table 3.1   Percentage of Trade Unionists in the Labour Force, 1969–76

	Labour force	Trade Unionists	Density of unionism (%)
1969	23,603,000	10,472,000	44.4
1970	23,446,000	11,179,000	47.7
1971	23,231,000	11,127,000	47.9
1972	23,303,000	11,349,000	49.4
1973	23,592,000	11,444,000	49.2
1974	23,689,000	11,755,000	50.4
1975	23,339,000	12,184,000	51.7
1976	23,713,000	12,376,000	52.1

Source: Taylor (1980) p.25.

Trade union density increased from 44.4% in 1968 to 52.1% in 1976, reflecting among other things the spread of unionism among white-collar workers (union density here increased from 29.6% in 1964 to 39.4% in 1974, a growth in actual members of 1.5 million) and among women workers (density figures here rose from 26.3%

to 34% over the same period). 'Unionism advanced in local government and education, in insurance, banking and finance and, most impressively, in national government and the health services' (Cronin 1984, p.190). In fact, overall, 'the late 1960s and early 1970s constitute one of the great periods of expansion for the British trade union movement, similar in magnitude to the growth between 1911 and 1913, in the early 1920s before the onset of the inter-war depression, and the 1940s' (Taylor 1980, p.25). And this happened in spite of the redistribution of the labour force towards those sectors in which unionism was traditionally weak, and away from those in which it was traditionally strong. In 29 of the 35 industry groups listed in Bain and Price's study of union growth in this period, union density increased, and in only five did it fall (Price and Bain, 1983, pp.342–3).

Thus the second consequence of a decade of the politicisation of industrial relations was the emergence of the unions as bigger and stronger both industrially and organisationally—bigger indeed than at any time in their history to that date.

The third and major reaction to state policy was the spread of militancy itself. The number, duration and size of strikes rose in a way unprecedented for nearly half a century. The change in militancy occurred in two stages, as Richard Hyman noted at the time:

> From the end of the war until the late 1960s the number of recorded strikes each year was close to 2,000. . . . Then occurred the sudden leap to the 1970 peak, followed by a fall-back to just over the 2,000 mark. For this 'strike explosion' a surge in stoppages over claims for wage increases was wholly responsible: there was no rise in strikes for other causes. It is significant that this coincided with an unprecedented acceleration in the size of wage increases. . . . while the number of recorded strikes fell after 1970, striker-days continued to rise—to almost 24 million in 1972, well above any year since the General Strike. These divergent trends reflected a sharp increase in the average length of strikes—from a few days to over a fortnight—partly a freak of two big disputes (of post office workers and miners) but also a consequence of a marked increase in comparatively long disputes . . . these averaged about five a year in the early 1960s, but numbered about twenty a year by the end of the decade. (Hyman 1973, p.102)

Richard Hyman's figures are given in Table 3.2.

Table 3.2   Industrial Disputes, 1960–72

	Number of strikes	Workers involved (000s)	Striker days (000s)
1960	2,832	814	3,024
1961	2,686	771	3,046
1962	2,449	4,420	5,798
1963	2,068	590	1,755
1964	2,524	872	2,277
1965	2,354	868	2,925
1966	1,937	530	2,398
1967	2,116	731	2,787
1968	2,378	2,255	4,690
1969	3,116	1,654	6,846
1970	3,906	1,793	10,980
1971	2,228	1,171	13,551
1972	2,470	1,705	23,904

Source: Hyman (1973) p.103.

The Labour Government's incomes policies were defeated in 1969 and 1970 by a wave of strikes among low-paid workers in local government. These were followed in 1970 and 1971 by resistance to the Heath Government's industrial policy, and particularly its willingness to tolerate the collapse of 'lame duck' industries and the associated unemployment. The new tactic of the 'sit-in' emerged—with factory occupations spreading more generally after their first successful use by shipyard workers at Upper Clyde Shipbuilders in 1971. The tactic of the 'flying picket' was to follow, with even greater success, in the miners' strike of 1972. And then, when the National Industrial Relations Court began to fine workers, sequestrate union funds and insist on cooling-off periods and compulsory strike ballots, workers responded by continuing to black goods (in the Liverpool docks), by voting to strike in increasing numbers (especially on the railways), by defending their imprisoned colleagues with mass walk-outs (in the London docks) and by being prepared for a general industrial strike against the hated legislation. As wage demands escalated, new demands came too—reflecting the greater self-confidence of a now more fully mobilised working class. 'Strikes over issues concerning personal autonomy—over fights with foremen for instance—became more common, as did other challenges to managerial authority. Sympathy strikes, though not large in numbers, seem to have entered into workers' expanded repertoire of struggle for the first time in decades' (Cronin 1984, p.191; see also Crouch 1978, pp.214–20). Of course it remained the case that this outburst of militancy was still heavily concentrated in just a few industries: 'at least a quarter of the stoppages, and a third of the working days lost as a result, occurred in five areas: coal mining, the docks, car manufacture, shipbuilding and iron and steel' (Taylor 1980, p.42); and that 97% of all workplaces in the manufacturing sector remained free of strikes throughout this period. But nonetheless a dramatic change had occurred in the pattern, incidence and scale of strikes; and it was in this sense that, far from solving the 'English disease', the Industrial Relations Act, and the government policies which had preceded it, made it significantly worse, by precipitating an unprecedented wave of industrial disputes.

Table 3.2 gives the figures of industrial disputes to 1972 in total, and makes clear the pattern of growth. But what it does not demonstrate so clearly are other key features of the militancy of this period. The first of these is the range of workers striking for the first time, of which 'three groups can be distinguished: public employees, who have traditionally been reluctant to take strike action; sections of workers among whom trade unionism itself is new; and what has been termed the "organised–unorganised": traditionally unionised workers among whom rank-and-file activism has never previously developed or has been suppressed by a union leadership committed to industrial pacifism' (Hyman 1973, p.102). Teachers are a good example of the first group, seamen of the third. Overall 'workers who had not struck since 1926 came out: blastfurnacemen, postmen, dustmen, women cleaners, farm workers, hospital attendants, nurses, teachers, all mobilised for the first time' (ibid.).

As militancy spread into traditionally quiet sectors of the labour force, the weight of strikes shifted towards official confrontation. The second feature of the militancy of the early 1970s which the figures above do not indicate is the changing involvement of national trade union leadership. In the mid-1960s, as we saw earlier, 95% of all strikes were unofficial, with union officers not directly involved. 'Up to the middle 1960s . . . union leaders often attempted to play a neutral role in major unofficial stoppages: perhaps formally (in order to placate employers) dissociating themselves from their members' "unconstitutional" action, but making little serious attempt to get them back to work' (Hyman 1973, p.107). But by 1970–71 unions were more officially involved, and the proportion of strikes 'known to be official' roughly doubled. 'While the number of short strikes began to drop, the number of national and official confrontations in the public sector rose sharply. Between 1964 and 1966, for every official strike backed by the union, there were thirty unofficial ones without union blessing. By 1971 that ratio had fallen to one in 12, and it dropped further still in 1972 and 1973' (Taylor 1980, p.40).

By then the TUC itself was heavily engaged in an extensive campaign to defeat the 1971 Industrial Relations Act. So threatened did the union leadership feel by the terms of the new Act that it was prepared to countenance—really for the first time since the 1920s—limited industrial action in pursuit of a general political goal. The TUC sponsored two one-day national strikes against the 1971 Act, and went so far (in 1971) as to instruct affiliated unions not to register under its terms, on pain of suspension. Indeed:

> by the time the Act came into operation, the great majority of unions were pledged to deregister (most being already registered under an 1871 Act). Several large unions nevertheless did not take active steps to deregister, either because membership ballots were not sufficiently favourable, or in order to wait and see what would happen. The widespread reactions over the jailing of five dockers finally persuaded the last of the large, holdout unions—the electricians—to deregister, and by the 1972 Congress the TUC felt sufficiently sure of itself to suspend 32 unions for registering, although these represented only 5% of total membership.
>   (Engleman and Thomson 1974, p.134)

This is not to argue, of course, that the sequence of government policy initiatives in the 1960s qualitatively altered the nature of trade union leadership in Britain. On the contrary: the quality of resistance of union leaders first to incomes policy, then to productivity bargaining, and finally to new legislation, remained throughout ambiguous and limited. Caught by their acceptance of the government's right to specify the 'national interest', and weakened between 1964 and 1970 by their traditional loyalty to the

Labour Party, union leaders initially co-operated in the formulation of incomes norms and persisted in their willingness to meet and discuss economic policy with ministers of either party. As Richard Hyman observed at the time:

> Fear of confrontation with government has been a constant factor in recent British industrial relations. This has entailed that where government policies have threatened working class interests, union leaders have either acquiesced in or, if opposing, have denied the political significance of their opposition and have narrowly confined the form of its expression—thus inhibiting the mobilisation of rank and file action which alone could make the opposition effective. This was the case with union attitudes to Labour's income policy . . . and also to Labour's proposals for trade union and strike legislation. In both contexts, the TUC agreed to institute its *own* machinery to achieve the aim of restraining wage claims and controlling strikes; in neither case was any serious effort made to contest the government's basic perspective of treating strikes and wage claims as serious economic problems which must 'in the national interest' be contained.   (Hyman 1973, pp.122–3)

Only rising industrial militancy among union members, and the seriousness of the threat posed to official trade unionism by the National Industrial Relations Court, galvanised official trade union opposition. To quote Richard Hyman again: 'what appears to have been occurring is a gradual recognition by union officialdom that attempts to suppress rank and file militancy may prove unsuccessful and merely discredit their own position in the eyes of members and employers alike' (p.108). For those reasons—and those alone—union leaders did abandon briefly their conventional preference for quiet negotiations and committee room agreements, developing a 'controlled militancy' in their attempt to block the Industrial Relations Act. When that had been done, by 1972, the union leadership then quickly turned again to tripartite negotiations with the Heath Government and the CBI, preferring that route to any further escalation of the industrial struggle. There was a moment in 1972 when union power looked capable of totally destroying the Heath Government; and from that both the Government and the union leadership were happy to *retreat together*. For the succession of government initiatives from 1962 did not 'revolutionise' trade union leadership in Britain. It simply forced it into greater defensive industrial militancy and political campaigning; to create a pattern of strike activity which, beginning as unofficial, came by 1972 to be dominated by official national stoppages (by post office workers and miners) and to include officially-sponsored national political strikes for the first time.*

A third feature of the pattern of militancy emerging by the early 1970s was the central role played by public sector workers in these struggles. 'During 1964–68 there were only 135 strikes involving just over 35,000 workers in the public services, but from 1969 to 1973 there occurred 347 strikes, bringing out 744,000 strikers for a total of 2,475,000 working days, an increase of more than seven times' (Cronin 1984, p.190). Professionals within the state sector went on strike for the first time in the 1960s. The teachers are a case in point: forming COPPSO in 1962, joining the TUC by 1970, and engaging in full-scale industrial militancy by 1968 (see Coates 1972, Chapters 6 and 8). The low-paid in the public sector also demonstrated a growing willingness to take industrial action. By 1969 strikes were occurring among public sector manual workers, firemen and dustmen. The miners too returned to their more militant ways; and indeed their renewed militancy after the toleration for a decade of industrial contraction was in the end to prove the most significant change of all. Deprived of their traditional control over the pace and method of working by the introduction of long-wall machine cutting and measured day work (the latter in the National Power Loading Agreement of 1966), and then forced to accept a 3% cut in their real wages between 1967 and 1971, a series of first unofficial, and later official, national stoppages by miners in 1969, 1970 and 1972 eventually shook the entire political establishment to its foundation.

---

* As readers in Northern Ireland will be only too well aware, scholarship on industrial relations in the United Kingdom tends to be focused almost exclusively on mainland Britain. It should be noted that the most successful political strike ever carried out in the United Kingdom came in May 1974, in Ulster. Then strikes by Protestant workers ended the power-sharing Executive peopled by representatives of both the Catholic and Protestant communities in Northern Ireland. This strike is excluded from the story here because its determinants lie entirely away from the capital–labour–state relationship with which this study is concerned. Nonetheless, we must remember that it 'ranks alongside the miners' strike of 1974 in being the only strike in Britain to have ended with the resignation of a government' (Crouch 1978, p.250).

The politicisation of industrial relations had—in the space of a decade—inspired larger and larger numbers of workers to join unions, to develop shopfloor organisation, to unite in the TUC, and to contemplate (and when pushed, to undertake) strike action. By 1973 the enhanced strength and militancy of workers had totally blocked the first phase of State policy, and had forced the Heath Government to reconsider its entire strategy. Indeed, the strike wave of 1968–72, 'with its climactic aftermath in the winter of 1973–74', beyond being possibly 'the most important domestic event, or series of events, in post-war British history', also 'forced upon the whole of society the recognition that Britain in the 1960s and 1970s was a very different place from what it had been just after the war, and . . . therefore pushed politicians, union leaders and employers into beginning the search for new policies, new programmes and new forms of social and political organisation' (Cronin 1984, pp.191–2).

In effect, working class militancy left the Heath Government, and the Labour Government which followed, with only a limited range of basic strategic choices. It offered them the possibility, in designing industrial and social strategy, of harnessing this industrial militancy for radical political ends. Or they could instead, if this was too daunting a task, attempt a second strategy, of co-opting and subordinating working class militancy to a more moderate national project. Or finally, they could quite simply reject the post-war settlement in its totality, and instead challenge and break the pattern of militancy and the organisations on which it rested. The tragedy, for progressive forces in contemporary Britain, is that a political party strong enough to capitalise on that first strategy was unavailable in 1973, and indeed remains so; and that the last decade and a half has seen instead the working out of the contradictions of the other two strategies. It is to the detail of that to which we must now turn.

4

From Corporatism to the Crisis of Labour

The first political beneficiary of this unprecedented explosion of industrial militancy was the Labour Party. Labour, in the relative safety of Opposition between 1970 and 1974, was able to readjust its policies without the loss of face that accompanied the Heath Government's equivalent 'U turn' in 1972. For the huge claims made for the Industrial Relations Act—that it would remove industrial strife and create the conditions for a rapid strengthening of the economy's competitive position—were totally discredited by the militancy which the Act provoked, and by the ability of small maverick employers to force the pace of industrial confrontation by their appeal to the National Industrial Relations Court. The Heath Government soon became a helpless observer of the anarchy produced by its own creation: and in return for effectively suspending its new legislation, drew the TUC back into negotiations on incomes policy and on extensive state aid to industry. In the event, agreement with the TUC proved illusive. The unions were in no mood to co-operate with a government that had attacked them so ferociously; and the miners in particular proved a stumbling block over which, in 1974, the Heath Government fell to electoral defeat. The 1973–4 miners' strike, the three-day week to which it gave rise, and the subsequent General Election fought on the question of trade union power, brought a minority Labour Government back into office—a Labour

Government which was armed with a political programme uniquely sensitive to trade union requirements and policy concerns (for full details, see Coates 1980, *passim*).

For the industrial militancy of the 1968–74 period had done more than discredit first a Labour and then a Conservative Government. It had also brought into national office a generation of left-wing trade union leaders who were determined to avoid any repetition of the growing estrangement of Labour and the unions that had characterised the latter years of the first Wilson governments. Through a newly-created Liaison Committee of TUC General Council members, representatives of the Labour Party's National Executive Committee, and politicians from Labour's Shadow Cabinet, these new left-wing trade union leaders persuaded the Parliamentary Labour Party to adopt its most radical programme since the 1930s. The Labour Party—under trade union encouragement—entered office in 1974 committed to achieving 'a fundamental and irreversible shift in the balance of power and wealth in favour of working people and their families'.

This was to be achieved partly by a new social strategy of higher pensions, price controls, steeply progressive direct taxation and the return to full employment. It was also to be achieved by an Industry Act that would combine extensive public ownership at the level of individual firms (to be bought by a new National Enterprise Board) with the negotiation of Planning Agreements between the remaining large private firms, the government and the unions. The Labour Government was also committed to the introduction of a new Industrial Relations Act: one that would strengthen official trade unionism and act as the cornerstone of a close and detailed relationship between the unions and the Labour Government. In this way it was anticipated that industrial militancy would fade away, and an orderly system of wage rises re-emerge, in the wake of the Labour Government's creation of a more equal society in which trade union influence would be enhanced at both the political and industrial level. Firms signing Planning Agreements would have to involve trade unions in the drafting of those plans; and legislation was promised to introduce a measure of industrial democracy into all companies, whether signing Planning Agreements or not. The Government's new agencies of intervention—not just the National Enterprise Board but also the Manpower Services Commission to oversee training, and ACAS to arbitrate disputes—were to be run in a genuinely tripartite way, with union leaders in key executive posts; and the Government was to formulate its general policy in close liaison with both the TUC and the CBI. In other words, Labour came to power in 1974 committed to a radical and corporatist solution to Britain's industrial decline; and as a result the trade unions initially enjoyed a quite unique capacity to specify both the agenda and outcome of key policy decisions at national level.

I

In the early years of the Labour Government much of that radical promise seemed likely to be fulfilled. The incoming government settled with the miners, froze rents, increased pensions, funded a number of worker co-operatives, set up a commission to explore ways of extending industrial democracy, and promised both a new Industry Act (with Planning Agreements) and a new Trade Union Act to replace the 1971 disaster. A National Enterprise Board was created, with union leaders enjoying executive powers in a tripartite relationship with private employers and government appointees; and equivalent arrangements followed with both the Manpower Services Commission created by the Heath Government and the new Advisory, Conciliation and Arbitration Service, ACAS. A majority of activists in the trade union movement wanted Britain to withdraw from the European Economic Community, and a referendum on that was arranged for early in 1975. The new employment legislation, when it came, tried to give both workers and shop stewards a minimum 'floor of rights': extending trade union privileges, enhancing worker protection against unfair dismissal, and attempting to guarantee equal opportunities at work for women. In all, in fact, 'between 1974 and 1979 at least 10 major statutes were implemented dealing with trade unions and labour relations, health and safety, employment protection, occupational pensions, race and discrimination, equal pay and industrial strategy' (Fox 1985, p.393).

But thereafter things very quickly went wrong, and old patterns of union–state tension eventually reappeared. The anti-marketeers lost the referendum on EEC entry; and the opportunity created by this defeat for the Left was taken to move key opponents of Common Market membership (particularly Tony Benn) from the Department of Trade and Industry. His successors then watered down the radicalism incipient in the Planning Agreement system. In the next four years the Labour Government negotiated only two agreements (one with the National Coal Board, the other with Chrysler) neither of which qualitatively altered either the relationships of power inside the company or industry concerned, nor enabled new and more socially-sensitive criteria to guide the industrial strategy planned. There was some substance to the Planning Agreement in the Coal Industry—and in fact 'Plan for Coal' remained intact throughout the life of the Labour Government, to become an early target of the Thatcher Government's assault on union power in the 1980s. But the Chrysler Planning Agreement was a fiasco, with the company selling itself off to a French firm under the noses of an unknowing Labour Government, and with job losses continuing in Chrysler in spite of the negotiation of the Agreement. The proposals on industrial democracy which eventually emerged from the Bullock Commission proved to be extremely modest, and were in any case abandoned in the face of a vigorous CBI-led campaign. Industrial policy fell back on the old NEDC machinery, 'picking winners' in each industrial sector, and giving them state aid without that aid being made conditional either on promises of job creation or of power sharing with the unions. In the event the Labour Government was not able to regenerate British industry by this route. On the contrary: industrial output stagnated until 1978. The index of industrial production was still lower at the end of 1977 than it was during 'the three-day week' in 1974; and unemployment rose steadily for most of the Government's period of office. It peaked at 1.6 million for the UK as a whole in September 1977, and was still running at 1.3 million when the Labour Government lost power again in 1979.

But that loss of power in 1979 was the result of much more than the inadequacies of the Labour Government's Planning Agreements, or of its spinelessness in the face of CBI opposition to its modest proposals for power sharing in industry. Electoral defeat in 1979 was also the result of yet another sequence of sterling crises, incomes policies and winters of discontent. The question of incomes policy had been at the heart of the 'hidden agenda' of Labour Party–trade union negotiations between 1970 and 1974. No trade union leader could easily countenance agreement to incomes policy again after the experience of the 1960s, and no Labour politician could win votes by promising their re-introduction. So Labour leaders fell back on the hope—and it could have been no more than a hope—that the problem of wage drift would eventually solve itself in a climate of greater job security and social equality. By 1973 the tacitly agreed position in Labour circles was that workers would moderate their wage demands providing both that the Labour Government kept to its side of the 'social contract' and that workers were left free to come to restraint voluntarily, without either political encouragement or legal compulsion.

Labour entered office in 1974 emphasising that it alone had a special relationship with the unions which could avoid the confrontations of the Heath years; and initially at least the Cabinet left trade unions entirely free to settle their wage negotiations at whatever level they could. That level took its centre of gravity from the miners' settlement, and by November 1974 average wage agreements were a staggering 25% higher than 12 months before. Both the trade union leadership and the Labour Cabinet found this level unacceptable, but persisted in the belief that it would, by itself, soon begin to come down. But it did not; and the Government's own settlements did not help. On the contrary: between 1974 and 1975 the pay of public sector workers relative to the private sector improved dramatically. In April 1975, 500,000 civil servants negotiated an extra 32%, and 100,000 power workers 31%, to match the miners' 31% in March 1975 and to follow the postal workers' 24% and the gas manual workers' 34% earlier in the year. Settlements like these raised the growth of average earnings to twice the rate of growth of retail prices between the middle of 1974 and the middle of 1975 (Coates 1980, p.63) and brought ministerial demands for wage restraint to a new pitch.

It took a sterling crisis to tip the balance, in what was by then a recognisable pattern of 'events leading to incomes policy'. The long sequence of government warnings, each tougher than the last, culminated in a decision to make a stand over the next claim to be made. This was the NUR's decision to reject an arbitration offer of

28%. And behind the specific dispute, a run on sterling and talk of 'national insolvency' completed the job; so that in July 1975, with inflation touching 30%, a run on sterling forced the Labour Government's hand, and obliged it once again to seek trade union support for incomes restraint. It must be said, of course, that the presentation and formulation of incomes policy by this second set of Labour governments (led by Harold Wilson to 1976, and thereafter by James Callaghan) was far more sympathetic to the unions than the Wilson governments had been in the 1960s. The tone of many government speeches became, as in the 1960s, heavily managerialist; but this time without the same strident anti-unionism of the *In Place of Strife* period. As a result, even though trade union leaders were no longer able to block the arrival of incomes policy, they were at least allowed to shape its detail. So it was Jack Jones who insisted that the first incomes policy of these Labour governments should be a £6 flat-rate increase across the board (with nothing for those earning more than £8,000), just as it was the unions of the skilled (the AUEW in particular) who protected their differentials by a return to a percentage increase (of 4.5%) a year later. The Labour Chancellor of the Exchequer (Denis Healey) regularly and publicly traded budgetary policy for trade union restraint, as Labour Ministers desperately tried to keep the trade unions with them as they went down the incomes policy road again. All that this achieved, however, was the creation in the public mind of an image of trade union power, at the very moment when that power was actually able only to block slightly the cutbacks in government spending on welfare demanded by agencies such as the IMF, from which the Labour Government was obliged to borrow in December 1976.

The initial impact of the incomes policy was impressive. Average earnings in July 1975 were 27.4% higher than in July 1974, but thereafter earnings rose more slowly, and at less than the rate of increase of prices: by 13.9% between August 1975 and July 1976, and 9% under Stage 2. Stage 3 was less successful from the Government's point of view. Earnings rose faster than prices in that year, at 14.2% overall; and that rate of increase was maintained in Stage 4, after August 1978, although this time it was accompanied by bitter and prolonged strikes in both the public and the private sector which cost the Government a large amount of public support. For each stage of incomes policy was adopted, as between 1966 and 1970, with less and less enthusiasm by national trade union leadership, and each stage precipitated a greater degree of rank and file resistance.

In fact, Stages 1 and 2 of the policy met little resistance, and no officially-sanctioned strikes against them; so by August 1977 the Labour Government could legitimately claim that it had achieved a degree of working class co-operation over a long period that no Conservative Government could match, and had in the process cut back significantly the pressure of wages on industrial costs. Yet even as the second stage of the pay policy was being accepted by the trade union leadership in May 1976, the signs of the policy's internal decay were already looming. The processes which ate away at the loyalty of trade union officialdom, and undermined its credibility and role as advocate and enforcer of pay restraint, were the rising tide of the working class unemployed and the persistent fall in living standards that accompanied this. In 1975 union leaders had seen wage restraint as an alternative to mass unemployment—the choice they faced was between rising real wages and jobs for all. But as the choice became more clearly one between rising unemployment *and* wage restraint on the one hand, and the threat of even greater unemployment on the other, their willingness and ability to preside over further cuts in their members' living standards began to erode (see Coates 1980, pp.67–8).

By September 1977 unemployment in Britain stood at 1.37 million; and the gap between prices and earnings under Stage 2 was a staggering 8% (inflation was still running at 17%). This 8% gap was the largest ever recorded between prices and earnings since information on both was first published in the 1960s; and it brought an inevitable working class response. Sporadic protest began to build up even under Stage 2, often with skilled workers playing a crucial role. One million days were lost in strikes, involving about 200,000 workers, as early as January and February 1977. Skilled workers at Leyland cars then struck for eight weeks in March and April 1977 in reaction to the erosion of their skill differential relative to the earnings of the production workers in the same plant; and 1,700 shop stewards met in Birmingham during that strike to reject any notion of a third year of restraint. The TGWU conference in 1977 publicly repudiated Jack Jones' defence of further pay restraint; though in the end 12 million workers did settle within Stage 3 guidelines, if only after the defeat of one official national stoppage—an eight-week strike by firemen demanding a pay rise of 30% which the Labour Government rebuffed with the use of troops. But it was Stage 4, in the winter of 1978–79, that saw major working class resistance to incomes restraint. A nine-week strike at Fords in the autumn was settled at 17% (more than 3 times the norm), and this was followed by a flood of strikes in the public sector: strikes by train drivers, by civil servants, by low-paid workers in water and sewerage, by local government manual workers, by ambulancemen and by health service ancillary staff.

As a result, the Labour Government left office as it entered it: amid major industrial unrest. Only this time, it was unrest directed against its own incomes policies, not those of Mr Heath. In fact, the pay revolt of 1978–79 was on an even greater scale than the earlier one. The number of workers involved in strikes in January 1979 was the largest for any month since May 1968, and the number of working days lost the greatest since February 1974, at the height of the three-day week (see Table 4.1).

Table 4.1   Strike Trends, 1973–79

	Number of strikes	Number of workers involved	Days lost
1973	2,873	1,528,000	7,197,000
1974	2,922	1,626,000	14,750,000
1975	2,282	809,000	6,012,000
1976	2,016	668,000	3,284,000
1977	2,703	1,166,000	10,142,000
1978	2,471	1,042,000	9,405,000
1979	2,080	4,608,000	29,474,000

Source: Bain (1983) p.211.

In this way, the four years of wage restraint that gave British industry its breathing space also brought the Labour Government in the end industrial unrest and electoral defeat. As one stage of the incomes policy followed another (Stage 3 in 1977–8 had a 10% norm, Stage 4 in 1978–9 a 5% one, each fixed with greater and greater degrees of trade union opposition), the willingness of

Labour ministers to castigate trade unions and attack working class power increased. A Labour Prime Minister ended up urging trade unionists to cross picket lines during the lorry drivers' strike, a Labour Chancellor repeatedly lectured the unions on the evils of secondary picketing, and the Labour Cabinet as a whole persistently argued that high wage settlements threatened price stability, employment levels, and the possibility of adequate welfare provision. Indeed, the feature of secondary picketing which seemed to anger the Government most was that it succeeded—it actually shifted power away from management and government towards striking workers; and this was incompatible with a Labour Government's firm intention to hold wages down for a fourth year in the name of a wider national interest which seemed, year by year, to require unemployment, cuts in public spending, persistent income inequality and restrictions on the real purchasing power of the employed, including even the low-paid. The whole experience of Labour in power after 1974 made a mockery of its promise to shift class power *down* to working people and their families, and eroded the claim of Labour politicians that their special relationship with the trade unions could bring a high degree of national unity and economic growth. It could not do that.

It could not even, in the end, keep working class electoral support for the Labour Party intact. Instead, in the General Election which followed the 'winter of discontent', and for the first time, the Conservative Party made significant inroads into the votes of skilled and affluent workers of the kind that had provided Goldthorpe and Lockwood with their survey data in 1962. In 1979 these 'instrumentally inspired' Labour voters in the car factories of Luton switched their allegiance away from Labour to dislodge their sitting MP, the Labour Cabinet Minister Shirley Williams. As many as 33% of all trade unionists voted Conservative in 1979, as against 51% for Labour. The swing against Labour 'was 10–11% among skilled workers, and as high as 16% among younger working class men' (Crewe 1982, p.11), as 'Mrs Thatcher won particular backing among skilled manual workers in the Midlands and South-East of England who wanted to restore their eroded pay differentials and relativities' (Taylor 1982, p.208). Once more a Labour attempt to forge a corporatist alliance of industry and the unions for economic regeneration and social reform had gone sour; culminating not in the creation of a more democratic and socialist Britain but in rising unemployment, falling living standards, industrial unrest, and working class defections at the polls. So severe, indeed, was the defection this time that Labour's hold on its electoral base was seriously damaged; and Conservative politicians could begin once more to contemplate with satisfaction the possibility of Labour's permanent electoral demise.

II

The experience of Labour in power between 1974 and 1979 threw into question the viability of the class compact embodied in the post-war settlement, and the policies of Keynesianism and corporatism pursued to sustain it. For reasons which were not immediately obvious to the politicians caught in the crisis, it was suddenly no longer possible to guarantee full employment and price stability, rising living standards and industrial competitiveness, all at the same time. The Conservative Party saw this quickly, ejected Edward Heath, and devised an entirely new strategy, as we shall see; but the Labour Party could not move with such ease. For it could not easily admit that the whole basis of its post-war politics—its mobilisation of a coalition of interests between organised labour and private capital behind a common commitment to growth and employment—was now coming unstuck. True, by 1976, senior ministers were aware that the old policies were in ruins. That is why every study of the period rightly concedes the adoption of monetarist targets by Denis Healey, and quotes James Callaghan's speech to the 1976 Labour Party Conference that signalled this shift—the speech in which he said that we could no longer 'spend our way out of recession'.* But that

---

* 'We used to think that you could spend your way out of a recession, and increase expenditure by cutting taxes and boosting government expenditure. I tell you in all candour that that option no longer exists, and that in so far as it ever did exist, it only worked on each occasion since the War by injecting a bigger dose of inflation into the economy, followed by a higher level of unemployment as a next step' (James Callaghan, *Labour Party Conference Report*, 1976, p.188).

did not stop Callaghan's Government continuing with its incomes policies, and continuing to strike new deals with capital and with the unions. Submerged in the daily pressures of government, and with their own credibility at stake, Labour ministers could only appeal again and again to the trade unions for restraint; and were unable to see beyond trade union power to the more basic shifts in the capitalist world order which were rendering their political project anachronistic. Labour ministers intensified their corporatism as they abandoned their Keynesianism; and electoral defeat in 1979 was the price they (and we) paid for the fact that by then the one could not be sustained without the other.

The relationship between these two features of Labour policy—its Keynesianism and its corporatism—is of crucial importance to the sequence of government initiatives throughout the post-war years. There was a brief period in the 1950s when both the British and the international economies were growing with sufficient speed to allow British governments to withdraw to the margins of economic activity. That 'golden age', as we called it earlier, was still underpinned by large-scale government spending and economic activity: in an expanded public sector, in aid to industries (like cotton) in need of restructuring, and in the provision of welfare. But those years were the period of Keynesianism alone, when governments could guarantee full employment by indirectly controlling aggregate demand in the economy through tax changes and interest rate variations which involved no explicit pact with either organised business or the trade unions. Both were consulted, of course, and the spheres of influence of each were not politically challenged—the 'corporate bias' and 'cult of equilibrium' persisted, as we saw. But it was only when the international capitalist economy was not growing easily, or when the weakness of British industrial capital was too obvious for the State to ignore, that Keynesianism required supplementation by explicit tripartite agreements between the State and peak organisations of capital and labour. That 'corporatist' extension of the machinery of the State had seen Britain through the period of wartime mobilisation and immediate post-war reconstruction; and as we have seen it was also returned to incrementally after 1962 as the competitive weakness of British industry loomed into view. Labour's 'social contract' in 1974 can be understood as the culmination of this corporatist response; and its abandonment after 1974 (first in the form of the Labour Government draining from it any substantive concessions to the unions and later, after 1979, its replacement by Conservative monetarism)—its abandonment is witness both to how inappropriate it turned out to be as a strategy for resolving those competitive weaknesses, and how deep had run the transformation of the entire capitalist world order within which Keynesianism could no longer find a place.

For Keynesianism, as a 'national project for capital',* was one in which working class support for private capital accumulation was guaranteed by full employment, rising living standards and basic welfare provision. It worked for a generation after the war only because the rapid leap in labour productivity associated with the long post-war boom created the material conditions in which the mass of profits could grow, and wages rise, simultaneously— and in which the tendency of the rate of profit to fall could be held at bay by a quickening of the rate of exploitation. (On this, see Coates 1980, pp.162–76; and 1984b, pp.48–9). The conditions favourable to successful Keynesianism vanished everywhere in Late Capitalism by the mid-1970s, as the boom ended; and across the chancelleries of Europe and North America, Keynesianism bowed out to a new monetarism of the Right. Post-war Keynesian-

---

* This view of Keynesianism will be developed in full in the last chapter, when the question of hegemonic politics is discussed. This usage follows that of Bob Jessop:

Hegemony involves political, intellectual and moral leadership rather than the forcible imposition of the interests of the dominant class on dominated classes. Such leadership is exercised through the development of a national–popular project which specifies a set of policies or goals as being 'in the national interest'—policies or goals which actually serve the long-term interests of capital at the same time as they advance certain short-term, narrow economic and social interests and demands of subordinate groups. . . . as the nature of the accumulation process changes, there must be a succession of hegemonic projects seeking to adapt national–popular objectives to changing reproduction requirements. This can be seen in the transition from *liberal social imperialism* in the era of late nineteenth-century imperialism to the *Keynesian–welfare state project* associated with problems of demand management and social reproduction in the immediate post-war period. (Jessop 1983, pp.96–7)

ism had understood (and politicians using it had experienced) unemployment and inflation as alternatives. If unemployment was too high, aggregate demand had to rise. If prices were rising too quickly, aggregate demand had to fall. By 1974, however, unemployment and prices were rising together: and to that fusion Keynesianism had no obvious solution. Keynesian policies initiated against one side of the employment–inflation equation could only make the other side worse, for the world in which the two were alternatives had gone.

What had gone was the long post-war boom. Sustained economic growth in the capitalist part of the world system vanished in 1974, the victim of contradictions in the conditions which had hitherto sustained growth for more than two decades. As we saw earlier, the years of sustained growth in the capitalist bloc had rested on US military and economic predominance, on a system of fixed exchange rates based on America's willingness to export dollars (in the form of balance of payments deficits) and on the acceptability of those dollars elsewhere by economies keen to buy American goods.

By 1971 at the latest, that situation no longer applied. American dominance had allowed and encouraged Western European and Japanese industrial recoveries; but those recoveries meant that US goods no longer had such a market. Instead, dwindling American competitiveness and heavy military expenditure in Vietnam had left a stockpile of unwanted dollars in the central banks of Western Europe which forced a dollar devaluation and the collapse of the system of fixed exchange rates in 1971. By then, in any case, the concentration and centralisation of capital which American economic hegemony had facilitated had proceeded to such a level that big industrial and financial concerns—operating on the international scale—increasingly locked all the major capitalist economies together. So expansion in one brought parallel growth elsewhere, with a diminishing ability to even out the booms and slumps within one economy by export drives into another. This interlocking of industrial economies, and the world trade cycle it had recreated by the late 1960s, was already fuelling inflationary pressures in the world economy before the fall of the dollar. Inflation was then pushed further by the demands imposed on these multinational concerns by the rising power of a fully-employed labour force. The long post-war boom had relied for the motor of growth at its base on an unbroken supply of cheap labour: from the countryside, from the Third World, and from Western family units from which women were progressively moving into paid employment. By the late 1960s these supplies were drying up. Wage pressure was combining with intensifying international competition to squeeze profit margins and to jeopardise the viability of weaker capitalist firms and economies.

It was the Labour Party's misfortune to come to power at just the moment when the oil crisis which followed the Yom Kippur War had tipped the balance between the old expansionary forces and the new depressive ones, sending the whole capitalist bloc in 1974 into its first absolute fall in volumes of output and trade since 1948. It was Labour's misfortune to enter office too at the very moment when the balance of class forces within world capitalism had shifted, altering the character of the problems to which governments were obliged to respond. When labour was weak relative to capital, as in the 1930s, the system as a whole lacked demand; and Keynesianism had its time. But the full employment consequences of Keynesianism had now allowed labour to consolidate its power. Capital's problems had moved from the difficulties of selling goods to those of generating profits while making them: in the language of Marxist political economy, 'realisation' crises had been replaced by 'accumulation' ones: crises of under-consumption had given way to crises rooted in the changing 'organic composition of capital' (for this, see Coates 1985, *passim*). To these 'supply side' problems, Keynesianism had no solution; and governments seeking to resolve them, as the Labour Government was to do, were bound to come up against the enhanced power of workers which Keynesianism had indirectly facilitated.

In the emerging impasse of the 1970s, governments faced starker choices than they had for the two decades before. If private capital could not accumulate with existing levels of working class industrial power, then either private capital had to be transformed or working class power had to be cut. The basic incompatibility of interests between capital and labour here forced choice; and took off the agenda of national politics the possibility of any corporatist resolution of that choice. For corporatism, as we have seen, was wholly concerned with the formation and implementation of industrial consensus; and where interests clashed in this way, no such consensus could hope to be sustained. Corporatism failed in those circumstances precisely because it institutionalised the very class collaboration, and consolidated the very distribution of class power, which were formative of the economic decline it was supposed to answer. In such circumstances rapid economic growth, if achievable at all, required a dramatic change in class power in industry, either away from labour (as with Thatcherism) or from private capital (as with certain radical versions of the Labour Left's 'alternative economic strategy'). What it did not require was the incremental modification of industrial practices and state spending characteristic of corporatist decision making, where the entrenched private 'empires' of the participating parties could be altered, if at all, only at the margin.

Because of this basic shift in the nature of capitalism's contradiction—from a crisis of realisation to one of accumulation —corporatism anywhere in the capitalist bloc was difficult to sustain in the 1970s; and it was particularly difficult to handle where workers were especially strong. In those circumstances working class strength made disproportionately large inroads into the competitiveness of local industrial capital, creating a situation in which governments faced not simply strong workers but also extremely weak and vulnerable industry. In such a situation, governments faced a particularly stark choice since, if they temporised with labour, the weakness of their own industrial base would quickly intensify. In economies with that problem—and Britain's economy in the 1970s must be a prime example—a government either had to go—and go quickly—into a radical recasting of its economy's structure of industrial ownership (that is, go socialist in some form) or rapidly run into the need to reduce working class power. The Labour Government of 1974–79, as we saw, lacked the stomach for the first of these alternatives, and was electorally destroyed by the second. The significance here of Thatcherism, as we will see later, is that it recognised this choice and acted upon it. It was prepared to discipline labour. It was prepared to break decisively with Labour's corporatist configuration. The Labour Government, on the other hand, was not.

There is a long-term lesson here for the British labour movement: about the danger and brittleness of a corporatist solution to capitalist industrial decline. The danger is one of trade union incorporation, a danger that flows from the differential relationship of co-opted representatives to constituents on each side of the industrial divide. When the representatives of capital sit at the negotiating table with the unions and the State, they do not by their presence thereby weaken their constituents, who quietly go on organising production and buying labour as the talks proceed. The representatives of capital may eventually agree specifications of the terms of that production and purchase; but their presence in the negotiations by itself does not weaken capital, nor their agreements automatically bind it. Not so with the unions, where the power of labour is more intimately dependent on the quality of leadership to which it is subordinated. If union leaders sit to talk, the unions pause; and if they agree, their constituents have no independent structure from which to ignore or reverse the agreements made. So, even in easy times, the apparently formal equality of representation of capital and labour in the corridors of power obscures very real differences in the impact which that participation by representatives will have for the constituents who sent them. On this, Leo Panitch is very clear:

> Trade union power is based on the effectiveness of its collective organisation. But the power of capital is based on the control of the means of production, and this control is not transferred to the interest associations of business by individual firms. This means that these associations' incorporation via state structures is less significant for capital than is the incorporation of trade unions for labour, precisely because these associations play a less critical role for their class as agencies of struggle, of representation and of social control than do trade unions for their class. (Panitch 1986, p.191)

And, of course, corporatism never happens 'in easy times'. Capital will only negotiate with labour under duress, and in times of crisis. Then the brittleness of corporatism is soon there for all to see. For those are the very conditions in which capital cannot afford to make concessions to labour. On the contrary: its survival requires the intensification of the work bargain, and the shift of rewards from wages to profits. Union leaders agreeing to that will quickly lose their constituents, and union leaders refusing will soon lose their place in the corridors of power. The collapse of corporatism in crisis—either by management defection or by unofficial militancy 'sucking' reluctant union leaders out of negotiating chambers and on to the picket lines—is evidence of the brittleness of the whole corporatist project in a capitalist society. By anaesthetising rather than removing the basic cleavage of interest between capital and labour, by pushing that tension down to lower levels of decision making, corporatist structures in the industrial and economic planning spheres in the end inevitably fall victim to the contradictions they were created to suppress. Alan Booth has recently captured that contradiction particularly well, linking the emergence of corporatist initiatives to the existence of *national* economic difficulties, and corporatism's demise to the manner in which those national difficulties come to be overlaid by intensified *international* economic processes:

> In Britain corporatist structures appear to have . . . developed during periods of national economic difficulty. The main objective of these structures appears to have been to evolve a method of reducing the level of British costs and supporting the balance of payments without having to severely curtail domestic output at a time of expansion in the international economy. . . . When national economic problems have been overtaken by international crisis, corporatist structures have been . . . terminated to allow industrial and financial capital to respond rapidly to more intensive competitive pressures. This transition has been facilitated by . . . the relative weakness of organised labour at the moment of these downturns . . . Under these conditions, the trade unions and the tripartite system, under which their leaders wielded some influence, are both seen as impediments to necessary economic adjustments and in some sense responsible for the extent of depression and unemployment.   (Booth 1982, pp.219–20)

Indeed, because of the basic contradiction between capital and labour in such a system, corporatism can only work when it is not needed. It can only work when the conditions of accumulation are so easy that profits and wages can grow together; and when they can, tripartite negotiations have no role. But when international competition intensifies, profits fall and unemployment begins to rise, the rush to corporatism becomes part of the problem rather than part of its solution. For it helps to obscure for a while the fact that the crisis can only be solved by *shifting* class power: either to capital or to labour. The Conservatives saw that, adapted policies accordingly, and have been in office ever since. The Labour Party refused to face that same agenda, and remained caught in corporatist crisis until rejected at the polls. The Party is now trapped in Opposition because of its unwillingness to break decisively with its corporatist past, the contradictions of which come to haunt it in the run-up to each election.

III

If we are to grasp the full significance of the corporatist impasse for Labour politics, we need to examine its impact in detail on both the industrial and political wings of the Labour movement. Its impact on the political wing will be discussed in the last sections of the chapter, once we have examined the impact of corporatism on the public image and private reality of trade union power. For the Labour Government of 1974–79 left a lasting impression in the public mind of the trade unions exercising excessive amounts of political power whenever Labour is in power. In the middle years of the Labour Government opinion polls regularly cited trade union leaders (particularly Jack Jones) as the most powerful men in the country; and quite predictably the Conservative Party was able to capitalise on this in the 1970s, as in the 1960s, making much of the need to 'solve the union problem as the key to Britain's recovery' (the title of a pamphlet by Sir Keith Joseph, published in the run-up to the General Election in 1979). Tory critics of unionism laid particular emphasis on features of the union's corporatist relationship to the Labour Government: the privileged legal position which trade unions were said to enjoy, their lack of control over militant sections of their own rank and file, their 'outdated ideology' (Sir Keith again), their special place within the internal government of the Labour Party, and what Conservatives saw as their disastrous impact on the growth of industrial productivity.

Indeed, there were times in the mid-1970s when anti-union hysteria reached new and ever more bizarre heights; and though it all sounds strangely dated now, after a decade of Thatcherism and mass unemployment, it is worth recording here in detail, not least because the hysteria of that anti-unionism was itself one of the factors which helped to tip the balance of power against the unions by creating a climate of public opinion misinformed about them and hostile to their activities. My favourite (and by no means unrepresentative) outburst from that period came in—of all places—the *New Statesman* from ex-socialist Paul Johnson, who saw unions as the prime cause of the 'nation's misery', the prime architects of inflation and economic decline:

> Trade unions . . . have flatly declined to allow the smallest diminution of their power to press the sectional interests they represent. Indeed they have steadily, ruthlessly and indiscriminately sought to increase that power. And in recent years, and in particular in the last five years [this was in 1975] they have exhausted or beaten down any opposition and have finally succeeded in making themselves the arbiters of the British economy.
>
> The idea of a vast left-wing conspiracy within the trade union movement is a figment of right-wing imaginations. British trade unionism does not have sinister ideas. The trouble is that it has no ideas at all. Most of its leaders are perfectly well-meaning. Some are very intelligent. But the movement as a whole is dominated at all levels by the complacent, the conservative, the unimaginative, the lazy-minded, men soaked in old prejudices and habits of mind. Bourbons to the core, forgetting nothing, learning nothing, negative, obstructive, slow, dull, long-winded, unadventurous, immensely pleased with themselves, and quite determined to resist planned change of any kind. . . . Men ought to be judged by their record, and (their) record is contemptible. Smug and self-assured, oblivious of any criticism, they have encouraged British workers in habits and attitudes, in rules and procedures, in illusions and fantasies, which have turned the British working class into the coolies of the Western world, and Britain into a stinking, bankrupt, industrial slum.   (Johnson 1975, p. 652)

Of course, Paul Johnson's anti-union strictures did not arise in a vacuum. As we have seen, certain trade union leaders did have a significant impact on the policy-making process within the Labour Party between 1970 and 1974, and party policy in those years was sensitive to trade union pre-occupations in a way that would have been inconceivable only a decade before. Indeed, the initial version of the 'social contract' on which the Labour Party won the 1974 General Election must stand as a high-water mark of trade union political influence in the post-war years. The unions were not the only force pushing for that contract inside the Labour Party, but their support was vital to its adoption, and the resulting 'width' of trade union influence was as impressive as it was unusual. But it was unusual, and it didn't last. What lasted instead was the Labour Government's willingness to *consult* union leaders, and to concede to them (and to do so in public) the right to affect the *detail* of policy over the general drift of which, after 1975, the unions themselves steadily lost control. It was in this process that the *appearance* of trade union power remained intact as its *reality* evaporated.

This 'evaporation' was at its most obvious in the area of incomes control, the issue at the very centre of union–government relations between 1974 and 1979. It would be wrong to create the impression that all (or even the majority) of national trade union leaders were opposed to wage restraint in 1974. A significant minority were, and support for their arguments grew over the period of office as a whole. But the majority restricted their opposition in 1974 to any imposition of a nationally-binding wage norm, and certainly opposed any statutorily-based policy. What they hoped, as we saw, was that wage moderation would come voluntarily, as a result of the impact of Labour Government policy elsewhere; and that if it did not, it could be engineered from within the trade union movement. They looked to the Labour Government to redistribute wealth and income over the long term towards trade unionists and their families, and expected local union negotiators to restrain their demands in the short term to a level that would maintain (but not increase) real take-home pay. This was the general drift of TUC circulars to affiliated unions in the first twelve months of the Labour Government. But then, as we saw, TUC policy was forced to bend, and from July 1975 the TUC General Council was obliged to respond (more and then less co-operatively as time went by) to initiatives on incomes policy that were neither of its making nor to its liking.

Trade union leaders in general (and Jack Jones in particular) won significant victories on the details of those later incomes policies. But these victories—which helped to sustain the popular image of Jack Jones as 'the architect of the policy'—should not be allowed to obscure the extent of trade union failure here. There were actually important *defeats on detail*, too. In July 1975, union leaders failed to have price controls tightened. They could not stop the phasing out of food subsidies, and they did not win the level of flat-rate increase (£8–£10) for which they pressed. More generally, they could not prevent the Labour Government from attempting the exercise again on three successive occasions, nor stop the fall in real living standards and degrees of job security of their members with which the first two stages of the policy were associated. Instead, the bulk of the trade union movement gave its support, however reluctantly, to two years of pay restraint during which no official challenge to the policy was made through strike action, and in which, as we saw, the gap between the rate of inflation and of earnings came to be as high as 8%. Instead of enjoying a role as 'arbiters of the national economy', trade union leaders fell back to the role of loyal allies of a Labour Government under external financial pressure, and helped to restrain rank-and-file militancy for as long as they could.

Of course, by the third year of the policy, with the Labour Government still refusing to reflate the economy on TUC lines, and with unofficial militancy spreading, there was no longer any majority union or TUC support for a third round of pay restraint. But it should be noted that even under Stage 3 the TUC insisted on a rigid observation of the 12-month rule, refused to give more than token support to the official strike by the Firemen's Union, and pressed the National Union of Seamen not to break rank with its settlement in the autumn of 1976. Indeed, the very weakness of trade union resistance to Stage 3 may well have led Labour ministers to underestimate the degree of rank-and-file opposition to wages control that was building up in key sections of the union movement. In the end, official trade union opposition, and more importantly rank-and-file militancy at Fords and in the public sector, destroyed the viability of the policy, and in so doing underlined the veto power of union action in this critical area of government activity.

But the fact that strike action on this scale was necessary to block government policy is an indication of for how long, and to what degree, policy had moved against the tide of union voting and against the wishes of important sections of the trade union membership. Nor should that militancy—damaging as it was to the Labour Government in an election year—distract our attention entirely from the quite remarkable degree of political loyalty, industrial discipline and wage restraint orchestrated by the bulk of the trade union leadership in the years preceding the winter of discontent. The public haggling between Denis Healey and TUC leaders on the details of Stages 1 and 2 sustained a popular image of trade union power, and indeed reflected the capacity of unions to veto voluntary wage restraint; but it should not be allowed to obscure the quite remarkable degree to which trade union leaders were prepared to subordinate their policy (and restrain their opposition) to a Labour Government with which they were so closely identified.

This retreat on the question of incomes control is just the most obvious and important example of a general loss of influence by the trade unions over the development of economic policy in total after July 1975. The TUC repeatedly pressed for the systematic reflation of the economy (and reduction of unemployment) behind a carefully selected set of temporary import barriers and with greater state control of (and investment in) the private manufacturing sector. Union leaders did not win that. They did gain concessions on employment policy—periodic mini-packages that had a marginal impact on unemployment by slowing down the rate of increase of redundancies that government policy deliberately created. But they lacked leverage, and were in fact blocked by more powerful institutions and processes. Labour radicalism was literally drowned by economic problems which the trade unions didn't invent, didn't want, but couldn't prevent. If the industrial and political leaders of the labour movement remained united between 1974 and 1979, what increasingly held them together as the years passed was a shared sense of impotence in the face of inflation and stagnation, world recession and intensified international competition, rising oil prices and generalised unemployment, to which neither of them had an adequate solution.

This gap between the image of trade union power and the private reality of the unions' waning influence has already been noted by at least two serious and well-informed academic commentators on British trade union politics. Lewis Minkin, in refuting the thesis that the trade unions 'hijacked' the Labour Party in 1974, noted in an important *New Society* article as early as October 1978 that trade union pressure to implement agreed policy focused on only a narrow range of issues. 'The fact was that, apart from withdrawal from the EEC, the policies which those union leaders initiated and pushed were predominantly industrial —specifically concerning the free collective bargaining process, living standards, full employment and conditions of work' (Minkin, 1978, p.8). Leo Panitch later narrowed this list further, emphasising the fact that the Labour Government of the 1970s, 'far more than had been the case in 1964–70, showed a sanguine understanding of the unions' own priorities—that when push came to shove, the unions would insist on those policies in the social contract that pertained directly to industrial relations, and would exert less pressure when it came to the economic strategy' (Panitch 1986, p.120). In his view, union leaders were prepared to be impressed by the *form* of the Labour Government's radical economic strategy (that is, by the retention of the NEB, the existence of the Industry Act, the verbal commitment to planning agreements, and the terms of reference of the Bullock inquiry) while allowing the *substance* of that radicalism to be slowly drained away. On this argument, 'the fact that Michael Foot allowed the TUC to write its own ticket on industrial relations legislation served, in terms of the unions' own priorities, to cement the ties between the unions and the government at the same time as reactionary economic policies were pursued . . . the *defensive* priorities of the union movement in the context of the crisis were secured, in other words, at the *expense* of insisting on alternative, let alone socialist, economic policies' (ibid., p.121).

This was the TUC's real area of failure on pay and employment —its inability to persuade the Government to accept the kind of reflationary programmes that the TUC's Economic Review annually suggested. The fact that the TUC now drew up and published an alternative economic strategy was a measure of its growing role in government circles. But government policy did not follow TUC specifications, for all their publicity; and when it is also realised that the TUC's own set of demands, as late as February 1977, still left unemployment at over a million by the end of 1978, the limits of TUC power become clear. Union leaders accepted as targets levels of unemployment that would have been politically inconceivable only a decade earlier, and yet they could not even win the policy to achieve that from the Labour Government with which they claimed such a close and special relationship. So when reflation came, after November 1977, it came because of the easing of other constraints on the Labour Government. It was no consequence of TUC power, but a by-product of the strengthening of sterling and of cutbacks in government spending, to the last of which at least the TUC had offered ambiguous but undeniable opposition. TUC leaders could claim with some justice that unemployment would have been higher, and public spending cuts more severe, but for their pressure; but this *defensive and rearguard* action was quite different in kind and impact from the *positive aspirations* of TUC–Labour Government liaison embodied in the earlier stages of the social contract.

As a result, the period of Labour Government saw a fall in all the indicators which excessive trade union power might have been expected to raise. The seasonally adjusted figure for unemployment in Great Britain in February 1974 was 549,000. By September 1977, as we saw, it was 1,378,000; and it was still in the region of 1.3 million in May 1979. The real living standards of the employed fell by 5.5%, 1.6% and 1.1% in the three years 1974/5, 1975/6 and 1976/7, and though they recovered slightly in 1977/8 (by 9% overall) the average male worker, married with two children, still had 'a real take-home pay in September 1978 which was £3.50 less than in 1974, and almost £1 less in terms of real net weekly income (that is, taking account of increased transfer payments in 1977/8)' (Panitch 1986, p.119). The distribution of personal wealth actually moved away from the working class between 1974 and 1979. No progress was made on industrial democracy. The trade unions did gain improvements in their procedural powers and in the legal rights of workers; but on the substantive issues of employment, wealth and power the unions lost ground steadily. There is in that sense some truth in the remark that what characterised corporatism under Labour in the 1970s was an improvement in the procedures surrounding redundancy coupled with an increased opportunity for large numbers of workers to try out those procedures.

What the trade union leadership enjoyed under this Labour Government was not so much the power to determine the substantive drift of policy as the ability to participate in a new set of procedural rights which created the very impression of influence that the resulting drift of policy so often belied. Union leaders were consulted on a scale, and with a degree of publicity, never before seen in peacetime. From these consultations emerged, among other things, legislation bringing enhanced rights to individual workers. And at critical periods in the Labour Government's history, those consultations took the form of public negotiations with leading TUC members, to win their support for government initiatives. The close involvement of trade union leaders in consultation with Labour ministers helped to cement the already strong ties of personality and ideology between the two wings of the labour movement. But increasingly over time the substantive issues on the agenda of that consultation process were not placed there by trade union pressures. At best, union leaders enjoyed the power to choose the lesser of two evils in situations in which the alternatives were neither of their making nor choice, and in that way the potential of their new-found procedural powers was drained of its substance by the severity of the crisis which surrounded government and unions alike. The much-vaunted alliance between the two wings of the labour movement persisted, but its significance for policy waned as both ministers and union leaders stood immobile and impotent before a world whose major social and economic processes remained outside their own comprehension and control (Coates 1980, p.203).

Thus the evidence of the years of Labour Government will not sustain the view that the trade unions had become the 'arbiters of the national economy'; though to be more charitable to Paul Johnson than he possibly deserves, it can be said that this was perhaps less obvious in 1975 than it is now. The impact of key trade union figures on the agenda of political debate, and on the way in which that debate was then being resolved (in the form of legislative initiatives and white papers) brought union power to its peak, a legacy of the leverage of union leaders over Labour politicians in the years of Opposition, and of the very considerable degree of militancy which the policies of the Heath Government had stimulated. But after 1975 the union leadership had less and less impact on either the agenda of political debate or its resolution. Institutions representing industrial and particularly financial capital came to have greater sway, and a particular set of market forces (manifesting themselves in high rates of inflation, industrial stagnation, balance of payments deficits and a volatile currency) came to shape Labour Government policy in ways which trade union pressure could not gainsay. Far from controlling the drift of government economic or social policy—or even having a disproportionate influence upon it, as was undoubtedly briefly the case in 1974—trade union leaders came to find themselves confronted with 'difficult and unpleasant alternatives', as Len Murray put it to the 1975 Trades Union Congress, alternatives which they neither specified nor desired.

There are a number of conclusions to be drawn from this. One that is worth recording is that in politics publicity is never a good index of influence. At best it is an indicator of importance, not of leverage. Trade union leaders were important to this Labour Government because their support was essential to the smooth implementation of policy in key areas—and this gave union leaders access to government departments and a veto on specific issues. But even that veto was slow in coming. For so often under this Labour Government, trade union leaders were visible not because they were shaping policy but because they were advocating it, acting as unpaid assistants to the Government, using their credibility and status to persuade their members to go along with falling living standards and rising unemployment which neither they nor the Labour Government could prevent, and which ran entirely counter to that 'fundamental and irreversible shift in the balance of power and wealth in favour of working people and their families' to which the Labour Party and the trade unions had committed themselves in Opposition. If the 'social contract' of those Opposition years is to be taken as evidence of trade union political power in 1974 and 1975, the fate of subsequent versions of the social contract must also be taken as evidence. And there the shift of emphasis was unambiguous: from a series of specific policy proposals which strengthened the political and industrial rights of workers and their organisations, to a straightforward preoccupation with the control of wages and the enunciation of vague promises of social reform without any immediate bite.

It is the recognition of this which enables us to situate the true character of trade union power in British politics in the 1970s. For the 'difficult and unpleasant alternatives' to which Len Murray referred—alternatives which confronted Labour politicians no less forcefully than they did trade unionists—were choices created by the particular character of the capitalist crisis into which the world economy had slipped by the early 1970s, and which the particular competitive weakness of British industrial capital then compounded. Neither trade union leaders nor union members initiated those alternatives, but instead they had to *react* to an agenda of politics which specified greater unemployment or more inflation as alternatives, which contrasted profitability with the intensification of the work process, and which obliged politicians to choose between industrial competitiveness and more welfare provision. Trade union industrial and political pressure could tip the balance between unemployment and inflation, or between investment and labour exploitation, and might try to affect the trade-off between competitiveness and welfare. But it could not remove the choices themselves. Nor could it prevent any union resistance to one side of each choice having adverse consequences for the other—and it was the visibility of this last process which resulted in trade unions being blamed for inflation or for low investment when in reality the 'fault' was not theirs. For what coloured the whole trajectory of union political leverage in the 1970s was a deepening capitalist crisis whose resolution required (as capitalist crises always will) a significant rise in the rate of exploitation of labour. This left trade union leaders not so much with power as with a *paradox*. That paradox derived from the way in which the rate of growth of profits in the British economy, though determined by tendencies endemic to capitalist development, was inevitably tempered by the severity of the class struggles to which those tendencies gave rise. This meant that trade unionists, looking for a 'healthy' economy in which to bargain, were faced with the paradox that their strength as unions could impede the 'health' which they wished to foster.

It is worth remembering, when assessing the true nature of trade union power, that even in periods of rapid economic growth union negotiators are always subject to the danger that any success in the immediate period might (via its impact on costs, profits and investment) be bought at the price of more difficult bargaining conditions later. That contradiction is even starker when economic growth is missing: when, as for the British union movement in the 1970s, bargaining had to occur against the background of a comparatively weak economy, in which rates of investment were already low, exchange rates already unstable, and foreign competition already sufficiently intense to prevent the maintenance of full employment at existing levels of real pay. For what could trade union leaders do, trapped as they were in the midst of a weak capitalism? The overriding immediate pressure on them from their own rank and file was to maintain existing levels of pay and employment. Yet, as any survey of debates at the TUC makes clear, trade union leaders recognised the impossibility of sustaining even the status quo without a major restructuring of British capitalism which would, in the short term at least, have threatened jobs and living standards even more. TUC hesitation and powerlessness here reflected the recognition by trade union leaders of the real dilemmas faced by the Labour Government, and of the resulting danger that trade union resistance to falling living standards in the immediate period might block the restoration of British capitalism's competitive edge on which future living standards depended.

If that were not enough, trade unions in Britain in the 1970s also found themselves in a paradoxical political relationship with the Labour Government they had helped to elect. For if, when the Labour Party is in Opposition, union influence on policy making is enhanced by the unions' position in the party structure, in periods of Labour Government that structured connection between the two wings of the labour movement invariably works to the advantage of the Government itself. With Labour in power, a mixture of strong organisational loyalty, close personal connections and shared political perspectives leads trade union leaders to subordinate their aspirations (and those of their members) to the changing specifications of Labour Government policy. There can be no doubt that this occurred on a large scale between 1974 and 1979, and that it applied even to the 'left' trade union leaders elected after 1968. We can see that clearly in their dealings with ministers within the institutions of the Labour Party, and when dealing directly with the Cabinet as conventional pressure groups. In such dealings, the concern of even 'left' union leaders for 'the party's electoral viability, for its organisational coherence and preservation during times of crisis, and for the success and continuation of a Labour Government in office' (Minkin 1977, p.8) continued to act as a powerful force moderating trade union demands and shaping trade union reactions to government policy. So, too, did the fear of the Conservative alternative. Indeed, the weaker the Labour Government became politically, the more the loyalty of trade union leaders to it reduced the pressure they could bring to bear.

In this sense, the trade union leaders' loyalty to the Labour Party had paradoxical results. This loyalty encouraged trade union leaders to sustain the Labour Government at virtually any price, while the Labour Government's failure to control unemployment and inflation generated tensions among rank-and-file trade unionists which, had the Government been Conservative, the trade union leadership would have articulated more fully. It could not do so with a Labour Government, and especially one dependent on Liberal votes, without running the risk of seeing the feared Conservatives return to office. So the union leadership spent the last years of Labour Government visibly trapped: seeking (in the end in vain) to avoid any political embarrassment for a Government whose impotence in economic affairs was eroding its already weak electoral base, and yet under growing pressure to articulate industrial dissatisfactions to which that unreformed economy was giving rise. Between 1974 and 1979 the historic connections binding Labour politicians and union officialdom, the positive commitments of union leaders to the Labour Party, and the close links they enjoyed with Labour politicians, all left union leaders particularly prone to subordinate trade union demands to the general drift of government policy. The unusually close involvement of key union figures in policy making within the Labour Party in Opposition, and their regular and close consultation thereafter, drew those union leaders into a partial responsibility for, a sense of identification with, and a commitment to, the general drift of government policy. Far from acting as barriers to policy that added to unemployment and falling living standards, many union leaders were drawn into a recognition of how and why such a policy was occurring, and came to play the role of spokesmen for policies that were in some important sense 'theirs'. Disagreements persisted, of course, on the timing and necessity of reflation and import controls, but this does not seem to have removed the general sense of identification with the Government and its policies from the minds of the bulk of the trade union leadership.

So there are general lessons here about the dangers of corporatism for the unions. In the 1970s, and even under a Labour Government, corporatism quickly became a strategy for working class control. Trade union leaders who shared the Labour Government's mental universe and dominant perspectives quickly slipped into a subordinate role, conceding to the Government the right to specify national policy and treating the whole state apparatus as neutral between classes. As a result these union leaders quickly came under heavy pressure to re-organise themselves both organisationally and politically. Organisationally, the Labour Government pressured them to centralise their decision-making processes and to discipline their militants: 'to integrate lower levels of the movement—right down to the shop floor—

more effectively' (Panitch 1986, p.203). Politically, involvement in corporatist decision-making structures exposed trade union leadership to powerful forces of moderation and restraint. Caught between pressures to act as agencies of a supposedly friendly government, and as articulators of working class interests, union leaders got the worst of both worlds. Unable to keep control of the drift of government policy, they eventually estranged sections of their own membership, and were obliged to give unwilling leadership to industrial struggle.

Both by first participating in corporatist structures and then rebelling against them, the trade unions left themselves vulnerable to intense public criticism from the Right about their excessive involvement in political life. That in turn laid the ground for the re-entry to power of a Conservative Government which would take from the trade unions, not simply their influence over policy, but their right to participate in policy making at all. Conceding the *substantive* drift of policy in return for the protection of its *procedural* rights, the union leadership let in a government which was to deprive it of power both substantive and procedural. The corporatist exercise on which the Labour Government and trade unions embarked in 1974 had come into existence because of trade union industrial strength; but in its failure it not only left the Labour Party in Opposition again, it also dissipated the public support for trade unions through which the unions could have hoped to sustain their struggle in what was to become a qualitatively more difficult political climate.

IV

The political power of trade unionism in contemporary Britain was not, however, the only casualty of the failure of Labour's mildly corporatist experiment between 1974 and 1979. The major casualty of that failure was the Labour Party itself. The 1974–79 experience seriously dented the precarious hold of Labour on its working class vote, and initiated a sequence of electoral defeats from which the Party has not yet escaped. 1979 was bad enough:

1983 was worse. Labour's vote that year fell by 9.3%, 'the sharpest fall incurred by a major party at a single election since the war' (*Guardian*, 13.6.1983, p.5). In 1983, Labour's vote per candidate was at its lowest since 1900. Its share of the poll was its lowest since 1918; and its absolute vote, at under 9 million, was less than Labour had captured at any General Election since 1935. Less than four trade unionists in ten voted Labour in 1983; and more skilled workers voted Conservative than Labour that year for the first time since the war. Admittedly, as Table 4.2 shows, four years later Labour did recoup some of the 1979 and 1983 losses. In the 1987 General Election, the Party attracted an additional 3.2% of the vote, increased its seats by 20, and pulled back semi-skilled

Table 4.2   Labour Party Performance in Successive General Elections

	MPs elected	Total vote	% of poll won
1900	2	62,698	1.8
1906	29	323,195	5.9
1910 (Jan)	40	505,690	7.6
1910 (Dec)	42	370,802	7.1
1918	57	2,244,945	22.2
1922	142	4,236,733	29.5
1923*	191	4,348,379	30.5
1924	151	5,487,620	33.0
1929*	287	8,364,883	37.1
1931	46	6,362,561	30.6
1935	154	8,325,260	37.9
1945*	393	11,992,292	47.8
1950*	315	13,295,736	46.1
1951	295	13,948,385	48.8
1955	277	12,405,246	46.4
1959	258	12,216,166	43.8
1964*	317	12,205,606	44.1
1966*	363	13,064,951	47.9
1970	287	12,141,676	43.0
1974 (Feb)*	301	11,639,243	37.1
1974 (Oct)*	319	11,457,079	39.2
1979	269	11,532,218	37.0
1983	209	8,437,120	27.6
1987	227	10,033,633	30.8

Note: * Indicates that Labour forms the Government.

workers to its cause at twice the level of swing it achieved in the electorate as a whole. But skilled workers continued to slip away. In 1974 the Labour lead over the Conservatives among skilled workers had been 18% (49:31), but by 1987 the Conservative vote among skilled workers was actually 9% *greater* than the Labour vote. Only 34% of skilled workers voted Labour in 1987; and there could be no greater indicator than that of the degree to which Labour as an electoral force was still in crisis. In the absence either of an accidental Tory disaster or a major transformation of Labour fortunes under Neil Kinnock's leadership, it does still look as though 'the forward march of labour has been halted'.

There is already a large literature on why this 'forward march of Labour' has, at least temporarily, stopped. Much of it comes from different positions within the Labour Party itself and falls into the predictable divide of Left and Right. The argument within the Party turns primarily on the appropriateness or otherwise of particular sets of *policy*. Policy proposals have been cited as either too moderate or too radical, and electoral revival predicated on first shifting policy in the opposite direction. The Marxist historian, Eric Hobsbawm, has been an important focus for much of this debate; and because of that we will need to return in detail to his arguments in the last chapter. But before we consider the specificities of particular positions such as his, we need to observe certain of the general features of this vital debate. Two in particular deserve careful attention. The first is the propensity of especially those arguing the moderate case to see the problem of voter loss as one which is largely *given* to the Party from outside, rather than *created* by the Party from within. The other is the associated tendency to restrict both analysis and prescription to the level of choices between policies, and to leave unexplored more general questions of political strategy.

Moderate voices within the Labour Party these days, faced with the visible and persistent indifference of more and more workers to the Party and its politics, predictably tend to specify as barriers to electoral revival those elements within the Party which resist any realignment of policy with the existing conservatism of the electorate. The key to Labour's problems, we are repeatedly told, lies in the Party's episodic and vestigial radicalism, and not in its perennial and dominant moderation. Yet such a formulation, in spite of its superficial appeal to many Labour supporters, is ultimately inadequate because it lets the Labour Party too easily off the hook created for it (and for us) by the traditional moderation of its own politics. For if Labour's potential electorate is now conservative, the Party has helped to make it so: both by what it has done, and by what it has failed to do. That is the key lesson which needs to be extracted from the failure of Labour corporatism between 1974 and 1979. What needs to be grasped in all its complexity is the way in which Labour in power *helped to create* the hostile electoral universe from which there now seems no easy and quick escape. What needs to be understood is the extent to which the events of 1974–79, and the sequence of election defeats that followed, far from requiring still further bouts of Labour moderation, actually demonstrate the *inherent limitations* of the entire Labourist political project (and the progressive *fracturing* of the tenuous party–class relationship that Labourism had created)—limits and fracturing rooted in the very moderation which the Labour Right and Centre now wish to extend.

The crisis which beset the Labour Party between 1974 and 1979—and which indeed had been brewing during its years in government in the 1960s—ran much deeper than just the question of policies or the pursuit of votes, important as these were. The crisis actually touched on the viability of the whole Labourist project as the Labour Party had come to understand that project since 1945. The dating here is important. Before the war the Labour Party really had no viable project. It had its principles: its faith in parliamentarianism, its commitment to the law and to the constitution, its objection to the use of industrial power by workers for political ends, its belief in the capturability and malleability of the democratic state, its willingness to recognise the existence of a national interest which transcended the interests of classes, and its generalised preference for a socialist commonwealth instead of private capitalism. It also had its critique of that private capitalism. It objected on moral grounds to the inequality and mass deprivation of inter-war British society; and was appalled by the anarchy and illogicality of the economic decisions which flowed from the untrammelled dominance of market forces. But in the 1920s its leaders had no idea of how to leave that inequality and deprivation behind, nor how to contain the anarchy of the market. The Labour Party knew how *not* to do it. It would not be done by revolution, as its Communist rivals argued it had to be done. But quite what to do when in government was less obvious. In practice, Labour governments between the wars, being so desperate to reassure private capital of their 'responsibility', were extremely conservative in their policies; and they paid the price for their conservatism and impotence in the trauma of 1931.

To a party in such a policy impasse, Keynesianism came as a saving theory (as we saw in Chapter 2). It made Centre–Left politics viable. It gave the Labour Party something to do when in power. It offered a way of running and reforming capitalism simultaneously; and it 'granted a universalistic status to the interests of workers' (Przeworski 1985, p.37). Their demand for jobs and higher wages suddenly constituted the route to prosperity for all; and as a result Keynesianism was adopted, relatively quickly, as the dominant theoretical framework within which Labour Party leaders of the post-Attlee generation came to understand their politics. So the crisis of Keynesianism in the 1970s—the sudden inability of governments to manage the economy to full employment and price stability—was in consequence uniquely a crisis of confidence and project for the Labour Party and its national leadership. As Stuart Hall and his colleagues have argued, 'the crisis of the state in the 1970s was a crisis of the social democratic state' (Hall *et al.* 1978, pp.318–20). Labour is still in Opposition in large measure because it has not yet resolved that crisis.

Labour in fact has fallen victim to the inherent limitations of a strategy which seeks qualitative social change through the use of parliamentary institutions alone. Its electoral impasse in the 1980s has been largely created by the interplay of conservatism and radicalism within its own internal politics, and by the systematic depoliticisation of its own class base which has accompanied that. For Labour has always been caught between its desire to articulate the aspirations of the deprived and its keenness to run a State whose viability depends on the co-operation of the prosperous. That dilemma has long been visible to Labour Party socialists of a particular kind, and was perhaps put best by Michael Foot in his biography of Aneurin Bevan, when citing an argument put by Bevan in 1931:

> In opposition, the Labour Party is compelled, by the nature of the class struggle, to take up an alignment which hamstrings it when in office. A Party climbing to power by articulating the demands of the dispossessed must always wear a predatory visage to the property-owning class . . . although all the time its heart is tender with the promise of peaceful gradualism. It knows that the limited vision of the workers will behold only its outward appearance, but it hopes that the gods of private enterprise will look upon its heart. In either case, one must be deceived. To satisfy the workers, the Labour Party must fulfil the threat of its face, and so destroy the political conditions necessary to economic gradualism. To calm the fears of private enterprise it must betray its promise to the workers, and so lose their support.   (Foot 1962, pp.130–31)

Labour Parties get into office only when things are going wrong, when enough non-Labour voters switch temporarily to them in the pursuit of an alternative. It normally takes a world war, or a long economic decline, or a period of intense class struggle, to pitch Labour into power. Yet when they get there, articulating some degree of radicalism, Labour politicians find that the constraints on the State, barriers to the left-wing elements of their pro-gramme, are at their most acute. Businessmen are nervous. The pound is shaky. Profits are squeezed by working class power that needs to be reduced, not enhanced, if profits are to return. Labour politicians in such circumstances, and with varying degrees of alacrity and enthusiasm depending on their own personal politics, always in the end succumb to these conservative pressures in the pursuit of that elusive economic growth which alone, for them, can refuel the reforms to which they are genuinely committed. Labour governments begin radical, and go conservative: that seems to be a rule of Labour governments. As they go conservative, they both attack their own base (the industrial power of the working class), with electoral consequences to which we will come in a moment, and then alienate their own activists. But they also fail: that seems to be another rule of Labour governments. So the activists always have a chance to 'win' the party back, and to make the leaders promise to do better next time. The trajectory of Labour Party politics, therefore, is not unilinear: it is cyclical. It involves the rise and fall of first the moderates and then the radicals, but always against a background of diminishing enthusiasm for the whole exercise in the eyes of more and more of their electors.

Labour Party conservatism has two sources, not one. It derives not just from the experience of office (whose general terms we have just indicated), but also from the pursuit of marginal conservative voters. Here, too, the Labour Party failure to consolidate a radical electorate is itself a consequence of the form of politics into which the Party has settled. For Labour Party politics build no organic links between party activists and party electors. The labour movement is a movement only in name. The Labour Party has never created a socialist universe—of newspapers, clubs, communities and institutions—to fuse itself to its people. Like all social democratic parties, it has not built its appeal to its base on class lines. To do so would be to alienate the floating voter, and to raise the question of class constraints on the state machine which the Labour Party would capture and use. Instead, the Party has appealed to its voters 'not as workers, but as the . . . people, the nation, the poor, or simply as citizens', and in this way has, like social democratic parties elsewhere, decreased 'the salience of class as the basis for collective action' (Przeworski 1985, pp.78 and 108). Instead of consolidating a strong class movement behind it, to sustain its radicalism in office, the Labour Party has been satisfied to establish an episodic and ephemeral relationship between itself and its people, a relationship wholly mediated through the pursuit and registering of the vote.

The Labour Party has always understood its own politics as, at base, electoral and parliamentary, each understood and practiced in the most conventional and unadventurous sense. In consequence, and because wholly preoccupied with the electoral battle, the Labour Party has offered no extra-parliamentary leadership to, or indeed support for, a whole range of struggles that go on outside parliament and between elections. Indeed, its national leadership has always tended to distance itself from struggles of that sort, precisely because of the capacity of industrial militancy to alienate the 'floating voter' on whom the Party's electoral success depends. In this way—as we will see in the next chapter—Neil Kinnock's ambiguous attitude to the miners' strike was fully in accord with the characteristic and well-established attitude of Labour leaders to industrial disputes with political overtones. The Party leadership has always felt threatened by them, and wanted no part of them. It always wants them to end quickly, almost regardless of the terms of settlement; and the Party organisation has possessed no structure, nor any established set of practices, to enable it to connect its politics to these struggles, even when support for them among Party activists has been high.

Instead, the Labour Party as an organisation has stuck to its role as a narrowly-conceived electoral machine. As a presence at grass roots level, it has lain dormant between elections, only swinging into frenetic activity in the last three or four weeks before voting is to occur. In those moments it has insisted—always by implication and often quite explicitly—that everything else should be put on one side, and that the whole task of the Left be turned into door knocking and vote catching. Of course, the very fact that the Labour Party in the vast majority of constituencies hasn't crossed any doors since the last election tends to mean that fewer doors open to it, and that doors open to it with increasing indifference, except in circumstances of Tory crisis that the Labour Party itself can do little to precipitate. Not surprisingly, then, Labour majorities when they come tend to be accidental rather than created, and invariably prove to be as tenuous as they are fortuitous. And as they slip away, the growing resistance met by canvassers on the door seems only to encourage Labour's inveterate door knockers to knock even more frenetically, as though a better canvassing technique could resolve what is in fact a profound political weakness in the whole Labour Party strategy (on this, see Coates 1983b, pp.98–9).

As the electoral base of the Party has eroded, it is not just the moderate wing of the Labour coalition which has been 'beached'. Socialists within the Labour Party have become generally unpopular too. They too have failed to consolidate and bring with them a constituency of any size; and because they have not, the coalition of interests at the activist level within the Labour Party no longer *maps* accurately onto the electoral coalition that Labour must win. The Labour Party activists who won the elections of 1945 and 1950 were a coalition of trade unionists and the philanthropic sections of a professional middle class—the bearers of the 'new Liberalism' of the early 1900s. That middle class dominated the leadership of the 1945 Labour Government. The Prime Minister, Clement Attlee, was a typical example: Fabian in his conception of the role of experts, bureaucratic in his view of socialism, technocratic in his critique of capitalism.

That middle class has now largely gone, of course, a victim of the proletarianisation of the white-collar function in Late Capitalism and of the vast growth of public sector employment. It has been replaced in dominance within the current Labour Party by a new 'middle class Left' of college-trained teachers, social workers and administrators in the welfare bureaucracies of Labour's own post-war creation—the welfare state. As we will see in more detail in the last chapter, such people gave their support to Wilson's technocratic vision in 1964 and 1966, only subsequently to be radicalised by the events of 1968, by the Vietnam War, and by the return of mass unemployment in the 1970s. This new Left within the Labour Party—this 'lumpen polytechnic' as it is often disparagingly dismissed by its critics—proved to be more radical than the old: keen on extensive public ownership, on withdrawal from NATO, and on the need for an 'alternative economic strategy'. But the tragedy of this new Left has been its inability (except briefly in the early 1970s) to fuse its politics with those of the organised working class, as Clement Attlee's middle class had so effectively done. The middle class Left took the Labour Party off in a radical direction between 1979 and 1983, but it did not manage to take large numbers of working class Labour voters with it; and because it did not, it *compounded and accentuated* the electoral weakness of the Labour Party, and opened the door to yet greater working class defection to the Conservatives.

V

The question remains of why significant numbers of Labour voters—particularly skilled working class Labour voters—were by 1979 so reluctant to support Bennite radicalism. The answer to that question lies in part in the story we have now told: in the emergence after 1951 of a 'gap' between the Labour Party and its class base which the experience of pre-war depression, war-time mobilisation and immediate post-war reconstruction had temporarily narrowed. In an important sense, it does look as though key groups of manual workers largely lost interest in Labour politics—these politics stopped mattering to them in the way they had in the 1940s—during the prosperity of the 1950s. 'Do-it-yourself' local negotiations made questions of national political choice less and less vital for well-organised sections of the manual working class (particularly its skilled sections); and thirteen years of Conservative government left internal Labour Party debates of no interest to any but the committed. Even the popular enthusiasm for Attlee-type socialism (of public ownership, state planning and welfare provision) diminished rapidly in the 1950s, as people experienced the new publicly-owned industries as pretty similar to private ones, and if anything less efficient and more bureaucratic than the best in the private sector.

Much of the responsibility for that draining of support for nationalisation lies with the Attlee Government, and derives from the kind of public ownership it decided to adopt. Between 1945 and 1950 Labour restricted public ownership to old, worn-out, basic industries, left private capital in charge of the economy's dynamic sectors, and kept the managerial structures of the new publicly-owned industries frozen in the old capitalist mould. As a result, the state sector had already become unpopular in the eyes of most working people *before* the onset of economic decline. As Leo Panitch correctly observed, by the 1950s nationalised industries *were*:

> . . . bureaucratic, inefficient, and above all, distant from popular control in any meaningful sense of the term. This was as true for those workers employed by the state as it was for the clients of its services. The term 'public'—whether attached to enterprise, employees or service—became in this context a dirty word in Western political culture after a decade of denigration by businessmen, politicians and journalists of various political stripes. And although this denigration clearly represented an aspect of bourgeois strategy in the crisis that involved turning the screws on workers, women, radical and ethnic minorities and the poor, it came to have a popular resonance even among some members of these groups because it threw up images that related to their own alienation from the capitalist state.   (Panitch 1986, pp.40–41)

With public ownership of the old style already heavily unpopular by 1959, the Labour Party retreated from it, but in that retreat found no way of permanently and effectively linking its own programme to the interests of the new affluent workers and the emerging ranks of the white-collar proletariat. Instead of 'mobilising the increased material expectations and the growing sense of entitlement of ordinary people behind a programme of structural reform' (Cronin 1984, p.172), the Labour Party was simply the accidental beneficiary in the General Election of 1964 of a traditional, though by now highly instrumental, vote. People turned to Labour as things began to go wrong in the economy, because they had always voted Labour, and because Labour claimed to know the way out.

Subsequent Labour failures in office destroyed the viability of that claim; and the nature of that failure, involving as it did repeated Labour Government-led attacks on working class power and living standards, quite literally broke the loyalty of large numbers of workers to the Labour Party. The Wilson Government's squandering of its second chance—in 1974—just compounded that disillusionment; and this squandering is a legacy carried by Labour politicians still. For workers have heard Labour's promises before; and indeed are reminded of any they might have forgotten by an ever-attentive Tory press. Moreover, the national leadership of the Labour Party is still not offering a programme which is qualitatively different from those which failed so traumatically before; and because it is not, and because people remember and are reminded, Labour has still found no way of winning its people back—either in sufficient numbers or on a basis which would sustain any renewed bout of Labour radicalism.

Just the reverse is the case: Labour's failure to insulate its people against Conservative ideas, its inability to make a qualitative break with its own discredited past, and the way in which its politics create, and then frustrate, a highly instrumental approach to it by its own supporters, all this has left an enormous ideological chasm into which the Conservative Party under Margaret Thatcher has moved with great success. There is plenty of survey evidence to indicate the scale and character of that 'chasm'—evidence which was in place *well before* the Thatcher government arrived to set its own political agenda. Indeed, it is a measure of Labour's failure as a hegemonic political force that, even though it was in office for twelve of the fifteen years after 1964, it could not stop popular attitudes moving against central parts of its programme. That is clear in the results of one of the 1979 election studies, which monitored 'changes in opinion on many questions that were asked in identical forms in October 1974 and May 1979'. Such a monitoring found that in '17 questions that can be directly compared the electorate moved to a more right-wing average position on 15 and to the left only on the questions of increasing cash to the NHS' (Kavanagh 1985, pp.543–4). 'The brute evidence is that the rightward shift of the Conservative policy in the 1970s was at least matched by a similar shift in mass opinion' (Robertson 1984, p.236).

Moreover, even among Party voters, support for Labour Party policy steadily weakened between 1966 and 1979. The degree of identification felt for the Party by its supporters steadily diminished. 'In 1964 "very strong" identifiers made up 45% of all Labour partisans: by 1979 they made up only 27%. In the electorate as a whole their number has been halved: in 1964 one in five was an unswerving Labour loyalist; in 1979 only one in ten' (Crewe 1982, p.17). And this could not be explained by any pattern of age or class change in Labour's electorate. Identification with the Party diminished consistently in all sectors of its electorate, as a steadily diminishing number of manual workers chose to give it their support. The key shift which lay behind these figures was less social than ideological. Labour voters diminished in the intensity of their support, and declined in numbers, because of Labour's dwindling hold on their opinions and attitudes to key political issues and initiatives. By 1979, for example, manual workers, 'Labour's natural sympathisers, were on average slightly more in favour of Conservative than Labour proposals' (ibid., p.26) when their opinions were set against the proposals in each party's manifesto. In 1979 eight issue areas were particularly controversial: unemployment, industrial relations, public ownership, race relations, taxation, the EEC, and the welfare services. On all but the last two, 'the Conservative Party were more representative than the Labour Party of the views of the electorate as a whole', and were closer to the 'working class electorate and to the uncommitted and thus convertible Labour supporter' (ibid., p. 28).

Hostility to the EEC, and a willingness to prioritise welfare spending over tax cuts, were the only issues on which Labour was closer both to general opinion, and to working class opinion, than the Conservatives in 1979. And even here—on support for more spending on social services—support was weakening slightly in 1979. Crewe's figures suggest, at worst, a drop of as much as 28% in support for this issue among Labour identifiers in the electorate over the fifteen-year period up to 1979 (a drop from 89% to 61%). So, by 1979, and even before Thatcherism held centre stage, the nub of Labour's electoral problems had come to be 'the sheer *gulf* that separates the policies and principles of all wings of the Labour Party from what the public says it wants' (ibid., p.42). It is the existence of that gulf—in spite of years of Labour occupation of government—which stands as overwhelming evidence of the Party's failure to consolidate its hegemony in British politics: a failure which cleared the way for a powerful Conservative revival.

VI

With the wisdom of hindsight, it is possible to see that the Labour Party laid the ground for Thatcherism over a long period of time in a number of related but distinguishable ways. It did so, even when its politics were in the ascendancy, by the moderation of its break with the dominant assumptions and institutions of liberal capitalism which Thatcherism has recently recaptured as its own. For, as we will see in more detail in the last chapter, the Labour Party, both at its creation in 1900 and at its moment of greatest triumph in 1945, did more than inherit powerful capitalist institutions. It also faced widely-held and systematically articulated liberal assumptions—about the integrity of private property, the neutrality of market processes and the general desirability of private capital accumulation. From these, the Labour Party—even in its radical periods and certainly in its Keynesian corporatist ones—never decisively broke. Its politics always operated on the premises which Thatcherism was to colonise so effectively in the late 1970s: that national interests transcend class ones, that the purpose of policy is to encourage and reinforce traditional patterns of family and gender, and that communism is always a greater threat to individual freedom than is capitalism.

What Labour offered as 'socialism' was merely the *addition* of moderating institutions to this private capitalist base. Socialism in the Labour Party's hands involved nothing more than private ownership *plus* a supplementary state sector, a free market economy *plus* welfare underpinnings, and private capital accumulation *plus* greater trade union rights. Labour treated socialism, that is, as a compromise between conflicting value systems, principles of economic organisation, and conflicting classes. So, when that compromise failed to deliver either the material progress or the qualitative transformation in social experience that was promised, the ground was laid for a Thatcherite revival built on the premise that it was the 'additions' that were the problem, and the compromise itself which was at fault. By half-heartedly 'rolling forward' the State as the answer to capitalism's crisis, Labour prepared the ground on which the Conservatives under Margaret Thatcher could claim that it was the 'rolling forward' (and not capitalism) that created the crisis, that things were going wrong not because society was still insufficiently socialist but because it had already become too socialist.

That claim could well have been rebuffed if the new institutions of the Keynesian–corporatist era had qualitatively altered the life experience of Labour's electoral base, and had in so doing won their way into the 'common sense' of an entire set of classes. But in general they did not. Instead, the Labour Party prepared the ground for Thatcherite politics by the way that Labour governments discredited socialism in particular, and radicalism in general, by the gap between their promises and their achievements, and by the low-quality performance of the new institutions that Labour politics called forward. Only the National Health Service, of all Labour's creations, has won its way into the 'common sense' of wide sections of the community; and for that reason remains to this day 'the difficult area' for Thatcherite policies, vulnerable not to overnight confrontation but only to the (over the long term, equally dangerous) erosion of its viability by incremental underfunding and privatisation by stealth. Few of the other institutions of the Labour settlement made this impact, and won this degree of popular identification. Certainly over-bureaucratised welfare systems, and highly-centralised nationalised bankrupt industries did not; and because they did not, they provided no popular bulwark against the revival of right-wing exposés of the inadequacies of Keynesian corporatism in practice. As Leo Panitch put it:

> The very identification of socialism with the corporatist and
> bureaucratised practices of an increasingly cramped Keynesian
> welfare state certainly did create popular space for what finally
> became embodied in Thatcher's market populist appeal amidst a
> politically privatised and only instrumentally collectivist working
> class. The appeal of less taxation, law and order and chauvinism can
> be a strong one, even if only temporarily, when reformism has little
> else on offer.   (1986, pp.20–21)

Like all social democratic parties, Labour came to power in 1964
and again in 1974 emphasising its close and long-established links
with the organised working class, and claiming to represent the
interests of organised labour through some version of a 'social
contract'. But in power, as we saw, the Labour Party was obliged
to use its 'special relationship' with the trade unions, not to
advance trade union policy, but to discipline and subordinate
working class organisations and interests. To do that required, as
Stuart Hall observed, that 'the link class-to-party somehow be
redefined or dismantled' and replaced by an 'alternative articulation: people-to-government' mobilised behind a Labour
Government specification of 'the national interest'. But that
specification 'dissected the field of struggle differently from class-
to-party. It set Labour, at key moments of struggle—from the
strikes of 1966 right through to the . . . 5% norm—by definition
"on the side of the nation" against "sectional interests", "irrespon-
sible trade union power" etc, i.e. against the class . . .' (Hall 1983,
p.27). And in so doing it created a terrain on which Thatcherism,
'deploying the discourse of "nation" and "people" against "class"
and "union" with far greater vigour and popular appeal' (ibid.)
was able to sweep all before it.

The cumulative result of these failures by successive Labour
governments, and of this particular form of Labour politics, is that
the Left now faces a crisis of considerable proportions, and a
paradox of tragic dimensions. At the very moment when the
failure of Keynesian corporatism demonstrates that any Left
solution to Britain's economic decline will have to be a more
radical one (a breaking of the class compromise in favour of
workers), the popular experience of the inadequacies of
Keynesian corporatism has eroded popular support for radicalism
of just that kind. Key sections of Labour's traditional constituency
have proved vulnerable to a revitalised Conservatism at just the

moment when their support for radicalism is at its most essential. Any left-wing revival in the 1990s, therefore, requires that Labour puts its constituency together again, in the most difficult of ideological climates, amid a balance of class forces tipped against the Left by previous Labour governments no less than by the current Conservative one. That revival will not happen without major changes in Labour Party practice and in working class electoral response: and it will not happen either unless political forces on the Left in Britain are able to undo the impact on their constituency of more than a decade of strident Thatcherism. Indeed, if the Left is looking for an appropriate 'role model' for its own revival, it could do worse than look at its opposition. That is one reason why any analysis of British politics in the 1990s, before it can judge accurately the nature of the Left's task, needs to assess, and assess with great care, the Thatcherite impact in the 1980s on the politics of industrial relations in Britain.

5

The Politics of Industrial Relations under Thatcher

If the radicalism of a government is to be measured by the extent to which it is prepared to break with the dominant assumptions of the governments that have gone before it, then the Conservative Government that returned to office in 1979 must count among the most radical governments of the century. For Margaret Thatcher and the bulk of her cabinet colleagues entered office determined to pursue a significantly different set of policies to those which had constituted the corporatism of earlier Labour and Conservative administrations; and they entered office committed, too, to a set of ideas significantly at variance with those accepted as commonplace in ruling circles in Britain since 1945. The Thatcher Government believed in the value of *inequality*, in the desirability of *self-help* and the importance of *individuality*, and set its face against the egalitarian aspirations of the welfare state and the collective strength of organised trade unions. It accepted the idea that markets left to themselves perform better for all their participants than do markets subject to government direction and control; and it was convinced that economic decline, unemployment and inflation were all to be explained by the excessive role of successive post-war British governments. It recognised an important role for the State—abroad, in the protection of British interests, and at home in the maintenance of law and order; and interpreted that set of roles as involving intensified anti-communism and greater expenditure on both the military and the police. But in general the Thatcher Government set its face against government spending, and held to the view that people are better off, morally as well as materially, if their degree of dependence on government funds is diminished. In other words, the Thatcher Government came into office with a philosophy that contained elements which were distinctly 'liberal' in the nineteenth-century sense of that term—a philosophy of 'the free market and the strong state' (Gamble 1979, p.1)—one that was explicitly and definitely opposed to the corporatist institutions and dominant policy commitments of the post-war settlement.

It is not too far-fetched to talk of a philosophy here, for Thatcherism saw itself as charged with nothing less than altering the entire political 'common sense' of an age—with shifting the assumptions of political discussion away from the terrain of social democracy. Thatcherism began, as it remains, as 'the Great Moving Right Show' (Hall 1983), an important example of hegemonic politics in action. Indeed, the hegemonic nature of Thatcherism explains both its resilience and its impact. When Margaret Thatcher took up the leadership of the Conservative Party in 1975 the social democratic consensus was still intact. As we have seen, it was social democratic ideas 'to which people had become acclimatised: the taken for granted welfare state, mixed economy, incomes policy, corporatist bargaining and demand management. If you stood up at that time in a debate on the national economy and tried to justify neoclassical economics, or indeed monetarism, you would have been laughed out of court. Everyone who mattered was one kind of Keynesian or another' (Hall 1982a, p.9). Thatcherism changed all that.

'Between 1975 and 1979 an effective ideological crusade was waged by the radical Right', who 'seized on the notion of freedom . . . marked it off from equality . . . (and) contrasted it against a dim and dingy statism which they chained to the idea of social democracy in power' (ibid., p.14). The ideologues within the Conservative Party played with the equation of 'markets' and 'choice', tied both to 'freedom' and 'liberty', and set each against 'statism' and 'socialism'. In this way, they set out to 'shift the parameters of common sense', and 'pioneered a considerable swing towards authoritarian populism and reactionary ideas' (ibid., p.11). It is in this sense that Thatcherite politics must be understood as hegemonic. They were, and indeed remain, hegemonic in their conception and project: as Stuart Hall has noted, 'the aim is to struggle on several fronts at once, not on the economic-corporate one alone . . . based on the knowledge that, in order really to dominate and restructure a social formation, political, moral and intellectual leadership must be coupled to economic dominance. The Thatcherites know they must "win" in civil society as well as in the state' (Hall 1985, p.119).

In seeking that 'victory', the Conservatives under Margaret Thatcher have not made the mistake of breaking sharply with existing political languages. Instead they have played on real contradictions in social democracy (especially its bureaucratisation of the welfare networks and the visibility of its trade union support) to tap into a sense of unease which even Labour supporters have felt with the drift of Labour politics since 1976. Margaret Thatcher and her suppporters have used that unease to give traditional concerns with freedom and liberty, choice and individualism, a new and stridently anti-collectivist content. The liberal attitudes espoused by the present Government are very old ones. That is part of their potency in Conservative hands. They have been around a long time. Indeed, as we will see in greater detail in the last chapter, they first came to dominance during the mid-nineteenth century period of English industrial supremacy; and, though challenged later, as that supremacy was lost, by new ideological formations (from imperialism to communism) they have never been totally swept out of the popular consciousness even of the organised working class. For this reason the job of the new liberals within the Conservative Party in the 1970s was half done for them before they began. They did not have to *create* a popular liberal consciousness afresh. Rather, what Thatcherism had to do after 1975—and what it did so very well—was to *re-awaken* that liberalism, by attacking explicitly the 'veneer' of social democratic institutions and modifications with which Labour had overlaid it after 1945.

This Conservative attack on the post-war settlement was facilitated, as we have seen, by the failures of the Labour governments of the 1960s and 1970s. But it was made easier still by far more basic inter-connections between liberal ideas and capitalist institutions. Liberalism is always likely to be strong in mature capitalist societies, because its individualism, its treatment of markets as neutral allocators of resources, and its emphasis on competition, do tap *one* of capitalism's two faces. In what Marx called 'the noisy sphere of exchange' in capitalism, people do enjoy the 'freedom' to choose, do compete, do meet the market as an impersonal arbiter; and they do experience all this as free acting individuals. People can feel free, and in large measure equal, as they *buy*; and that is what liberalism emphasises. What they cannot do in capitalism, however, is feel either so free or so equal when they *work*. Liberalism fits well with the experience of the market place in capitalism, but not with the experience of the factory. For in the factory people experience the social relations of production that underpin the 'noisy sphere' of exchange,and in that area of social life—geared as it is to the production of the commodities that will later be so noisily exchanged—class inequalities drain that liberal sense of freedom and equality away for the majority.

Since under capitalism the social relationships of production are so unequal—and are unavoidably experienced as such by the majority of people caught up within them—liberalism rarely suffices as a stock of ideas through which to explain and legitimate the existing order. Liberalism leaves a 'space' in people's experience of inequality that radicals and socialists can normally exploit, and into which they can pour alternative frameworks of thought and models of social organisation. Liberalism can then revive only when the frameworks and models of radicalism are discredited, as they were in 1979. The skill of the Conservative Party under Margaret Thatcher after 1975 was to appeal to people not as producers, not as class-structured participants in highly unequal social relationships of production, but as consumers (of law and order, shares, tax cuts, wage goods and houses), enjoying and requiring the formal equality to choose and to compete. So deep and so traumatic had been Labour's failure to create an effective corporatist socialism based on producer groups that Margaret Thatcher's Conservatives were then able to persuade wider and wider sections of society that their 'freedom' as consumers could only be enhanced if the power of producer groups in the labour market was not merely frozen but was actually reduced. It was quite an achievement: to persuade the majority of the population that trade unions are a bad thing and private capitalist monopolies a good one, at the very time when capitalist concerns were leaving large numbers of people unemployed and were widening the gap between rich and poor. But the Conservative Party under Margaret Thatcher has got away with it, and in its success has gained for itself the political freedom to diminish significantly the power of trade unions both in industry and before the State.

Of course, any brief résumé of the overall character of Thatcherism runs the risk of making Conservative policy after 1979 seem more coherent and consistent than in reality it was, and may miss, unless it is careful, the *priorities within* Conservative policy that the differential pattern of consistency reflects. As Peter Riddell correctly warned us, 'both opponents and supporters of the Thatcher Administration have created more of a pattern from disconnected events and policies than is warranted' (Riddell 1983, p.16). It has to be remembered that the Conservative Party in 1979 was, and to a lesser degree remains, a coalition of contradictory political forces—some 'wet' and some 'dry'—and if the incremental rise of the 'dry' has all but removed the more Keynesian-minded ministers from the later Thatcher cabinets, that does not mean that the *focus* of Thatcherism has moved systematically to the Right after each General Election. On the contrary, Conservative policy has had its phases, with different emphases in each. 'Its first term was about extolling sacrifice, lowering expectations, and promoting the market. The second was about privatisation (which hardly figured in the first term) . . . the third' is proving to be 'about that still unconquered stronghold of social democracy, the welfare state' (Jacques 1987, p.10).

The first Thatcher Cabinet was officially committed to a monetarist view of economic policy, one that made control of the money supply vital to the war against inflation. Later Thatcherite cabinets slipped quietly away from that: retaining their commitment to market forces, but concentrating instead on the privatisation of larger and larger spheres of government activity as a more effective way of curbing the level and growth of government spending. Thatcherite Conservatives have been prepared to shift the emphases of their policy—to be flexible on detail—the better to keep their strategic objective intact. That objective has been, and remains, the dismantling of the post-war settlement: the removal of corporatist institutions, the diminution of the power of organised labour, and the creation of general social conditions which will block the rise of Labour again. On this, the underlying Thatcherite project, policy has been remarkably consistent since 1979. 'Once again, solving the trade union problem has become the key to the politics of capital' (Strinati 1983, p.85); and as a result the Conservative Party under Margaret Thatcher has been at its most coherent, consistent and unremitting in its handling of the politics of industrial relations.

In fact, Thatcherite policies on the question of labour have had a complex logic whose coherence derives from the way in which they constitute a coherent anti-corporatist strategy for the reconstitution of the economic strength and political dominance of capital in Britain. That logic has worked itself out in the way described below.

I

The first phase of the Thatcherite attempt permanently to shift the balance and character of class forces in favour of capital in Britain began before the 1979 General Election, and took the form of a major *ideological* onslaught on the role of trade unions. There is nothing new, of course, in Conservative denunciations of trade union power. Leading Conservatives have long been prone to refer to unions as trade*s* unions, in a tone which seems to offer the extra 's' as a kind of government health warning; and even before this became common practice, right-wing forces in Britain regularly used their control of the popular press to attack union power whenever this manifested itself. The depth of liberal assumptions in the popular consciousness (not least about the integrity of private property) has long enabled anti-trade union forces to present the exercise by unions of a limited defensive role as an illegitimate challenge to the 'freedom to manage'; and (as we saw in Chapter 4) the necessarily 'visible' and 'reactive' nature of trade unionism has equally left the labour movement vulnerable to condemnation as disruptive, violent and unconstitutional. So deeply held, indeed, are these views in right-wing circles in contemporary Britain that any show of trade union strength tends to generate not just resistance but something akin to hysteria—a 'levée en masse' of petit-bourgeois prejudice, as Edward Thompson once so graphically described it (Thompson 1980, p.39).

That mobilisation of right-wing *anger* at the 'effrontery' of trade unionism came to boiling point in 1974 and 1975, when the industrial militancy of the Heath years did give trade unionism, for a brief moment as we saw earlier, a larger than normal degree of influence on the specification of the national political agenda. This hysteria fed itself into, and was then orchestrated by, the rising tide of Thatcherism within the Conservative Party; and received one of its fullest statements in Sir Keith Joseph's 1979 pamphlet, which was appropriately named *Solving the Union Problem is the Key to Britain's Recovery*. Sir Keith's argument within that pamphlet, that 'union power should be reduced . . . because the present imbalance of power bars our way to national recovery', was fully in line with the bulk of public statements about trade unionism made by leading Conservative politicians both before and after 1979. Sir Keith:

'Our unions have been uniquely privileged for several decades . . . The predictable result has been the growing use of strikes and the strike threat. In a trade dispute most things seem permitted for the union side: breaking contracts, inducing others to break contracts, picketing of non-involved companies, secondary boycotts. A trade dispute can be between workers and workers; it can concern matters of discipline, membership, facilities; it may even relate to matters overseas. All this is unique in Britain; there is nothing like it in other countries.

As we would expect, this 'militants charter' . . . has bred militants, and driven moderates underground. Indeed, we are now seeing militants increasingly taking over control from union officials.

Union leaders, having in many cases failed to educate either themselves or their members, while winning for them excessive powers, have lost the ability to control them. National economic failure and the militants charter have given a supreme opportunity to the left-wing minority whose instincts are destructive, who are bitterly opposed to the free-enterprise economy which most people want. The result is growing confusion. Shop stewards disregard union officials; workers start to distrust shop stewards. Members strike when ordered by their unions to work, and—less often—work when ordered to strike.

We now face an unstable situation; the collapse of socialist expectations; increasingly ruthless efforts by big unions to escape the consequences; inter-union warfare; and the fruits of the militants charter. Politicians who urge restraint on union leaders, or who criticize their members for greed, ignore the forces at work.

To ask one union to sacrifice its own interests 'for the national good' without guarantee that other unions will do likewise is as unrealistic as it is to urge housewives not to anticipate a bread strike or motorists not to fill up before a petrol strike. The national good can be secured only by changing the framework, the rules of the game, and then ensuring that everyone plays fairly by them. That is what Margaret Thatcher has called for.

(Joseph 1979, cited in Coates and Hillard, 1986, pp.99–100)

Politicians espousing such views totally altered the political climate surrounding trade unionism. Trade union leaders found themselves expelled from the corridors of power. 'Government-initiated contacts, personal meetings and contacts with the Prime Minister, measures of closeness between groups and policy makers, all have declined (for the trade unions) under the Conservatives. Resort to lobbying and protest activity, measures of distance between groups and policy makers, have risen rapidly since 1979' (Mitchell 1987b, p.515).

Corporatist institutions were either closed down entirely (as was the National Enterprise Board), or downgraded in importance (like the National Economic Development Council, from which the trade unions themselves withdrew for a while in protest at government policy towards them). Not all the corporatist institutions were closed down immediately. The Health and Safety Executive managed to hang on, doing low key but vital protective work on a restricted budget. The MSC survived until 1988 when, having been renamed the Training Commission, it was suddenly shut down entirely after the TUC voted not to support its major training programme. The speed with which the Conservative Government took this opportunity to expel senior trade union figures from any executive influence over government policy on training was fully in line with its general determination to downgrade the whole apparatus of corporatist institutions which it inherited in 1979. Instead of being welcomed as junior partners in a corporatist strategy of economic regeneration, as they had been in differing degrees continuously since 1945, trade unions found themselves under attack in a climate in which the Conservatives were targeting their members as potential buyers of council houses,as recipients of law and order, as purchasers of shares in privatised industry, as beneficiaries of cuts in direct personal taxation, as proud nationalists watching military success in the South Atlantic, and as individuals in need of protection *against* the power of the unions to which, inexplicably, so many of them continued to belong.

The 'change of rules' to which Sir Keith Joseph earlier referred constituted a second stage in the Thatcherite attempt to shift class power away from organised labour. But on this occasion, and unlike 1971, changes were introduced over a number of years, in a series of statutes, piecemeal, drip by drip. And also, again unlike 1971, the Conservatives did succeed this time in significantly diminishing the capacity of trade unions to strike without liability to claims for civil damages by the employers with whom their members were in dispute. The *1980 Employment Act* was the first major piece of legislation here. This Act made secondary picketing illegal, and left union members engaging in sympathy strikes open to claims for damages by disgruntled employers. Under its terms legal protection for unions and their members was made available only for disputes with the immediate employer, or for secondary action focused exclusively on direct consumers or suppliers of that employer. Government money was made available, under the Act, to help finance union ballots on strikes, union elections and changes in union rules. The Act also gave the Secretary of State for Employment the right to draft Codes of Fair Industrial Relations Practice which, though not immediately enforceable by the courts, were available for use by judges and Industrial Tribunals. That power was used primarily to restrict to a derisory level the number of pickets legitimately able to enforce a strike call. The Code insisted that 'as a general rule it will be rare for such a number to exceed six, and frequently a smaller number will suffice' (cited in Saville 1986, pp.299–300); and in this way the 1980 Act and its Codes shifted the balance of legal rights firmly against mass picketing and broadly based industrial disputes. The Act also took away from unions the right to claim recognition from recalcitrant employers, or to claim 'the going rate from employers who were paying below the "recognised" or "general" level of terms and conditions' (MacInnes 1987, p.53) in their industry. It also extended from six months to two years the length of employment needed before a claim for unfair dismissal could be brought to an Industrial Tribunal; and it required an 80% vote of all the workers affected before a union could win a closed shop.

The *1982 Act* then went further, requiring periodic ballots on closed shops, and narrowing still more the definition of a trade dispute in which no claim for damages could be brought against the unions, to ones between workers and their employer 'wholly or mainly' about terms and conditions of employment. In this way, 'the definition of what was a "trade dispute" under the law was narrowed to outlaw disruption where none of the workers were in direct dispute themselves with their employer; disputes where workers were in conflict with their own unions; and those not wholly or mainly about pay, conditions and jobs or matters of an industrial character. This was a clear move to make solidarity actions and so-called political strikes unlawful' (Taylor 1987b, p.21). In effect, the 1982 Act left union funds vulnerable to claims for damages for actions that fell outside a very limited set of disputes, and allowed unions to be served with injunctions banning them from broader, and now 'unlawful' industrial action. The 1982 Act also banned industrial action against non-union companies, and outlawed clauses in contracts requiring the use of union labour; and under its terms employers could selectively dismiss strikers without this being grounds for appeals of 'unfair dismissal' before an Industrial Tribunal.

The *1984 Act* then switched the focus of reform away from the external behaviour of trade unions and their members, and towards the unions's internal practices. Arguing that the unions had become 'ossified oligarchies, out of touch with the changing moods of shopfloor life', the Government presented its changes as 'giving the unions back to their members' (Taylor 1987b, p.21). It insisted on secret ballots before strikes. It insisted on the regular re-election of union excutives by secret ballot; and it obliged unions with political funds to ballot their members on whether these should be retained. That last proposal, as we will see later, backfired when applied; but that one defeat has not stopped the Government from proposing recently effectively to outlaw the closed shop, to allow individual union members (and not just employers) to require secret ballots before strike action, and to enshrine in law the right of individual trade union members *not* to strike even when a majority vote in favour of strike action has been obtained. By 1987, that is, the whole legal framework around trade unionism had been shifted, to ensure that the vast majority of votes taken by unions would be postal and secret rather than mass and open, that trade union control of entry to the job via closed shops would be pushed back towards managements, and that the flying pickets and mass picketing strategies, used so effectively by unions during the Heath and Callaghan governments, would no longer be legal.

The justification often given for these changes, as we have just seen, was one of strengthening democracy, of 'safeguarding the liberty of the individual from the abuse of union power' as Conservative Employment Secretaries are prone to put it, and of 'improving the operation of the labour market by providing a balanced framework of industrial relations law' (Norman Tebbitt in 1982). 'Freedom' and 'balance' have been powerful themes in the litany throughout; but the freedom enhanced by those laws has been the freedom of capital, not labour, and the balance has been in reality the imbalance of class power played out through the stacked rules of the capitalist market. So the gap between rhetoric and reality here needs to be remembered, and the preoccupation of Conservative ministers with power relationships, and not individual rights, clearly understood. As Neil Mitchell has correctly observed:

> The claim by policy-makers that this legislation enhances democracy is . . . questionable. There is little evidence of substantial member-ship unrest over political funds or with the various internal decision-making processes used by unions before the legislation. Moreover, as has often been pointed out, there has been no corresponding legislation on corporate political contributions, that is, to make them subject to a specific shareholder ballot, which makes the 1984 Act appear to have more to do with undermining the political opposition than with democracy. The Industrial Society, which aims to speak for employers and unions, condemned the provisions of the 1984 Act as 'setting standards of democracy not demanded in any other sphere of life'. More important than democracy may be the belief that union members are less militant than union leaders. The 'personal conviction' clause allowing for individual exemptions from closed shops can be defended in terms of individual freedom, though to be consistent similar exceptions should apply to other collective decisions presumably including those of government. But weakening the closed shop also makes employees less able to counter-balance corporate power.   (Mitchell 1987a, p.37)

The real force of these Acts—to reduce union power, rather than to strengthen democratic processes in society as a whole—is

evident in many other initiatives taken by the Thatcher Government. The 1980 Act eroded rights to maternity leave and to wage
guarantees to workers laid off in a strike. In fact, 'ministers
believed that workers were pricing themselves out of jobs,
particularly at the youth end of the labour market, because of the
unrealistically high levels of union-negotiated wages and the
operation of the tripartite Wages Councils' (Taylor 1987b, p.22).
So in 1986 all workers under the age of 21 were taken out of the
jurisdiction of the Wages Councils. Moreover, and as early as
1980, in Clause 6 of that year's Social Security Bill, the
Government reduced by between £12 and £16 the total of weekly
benefit payable to the wives and dependants of workers on strike,
and removed the entitlement to benefit entirely from strikers
without wives or dependants. The Secretary of State for Health
and Social Security was very clear on the purpose of this change.
As he told the House of Commons in defence of his new Clause,
the Government was elected to, 'among other things, restore a
fairer bargaining balance between employers and trade unions.
Clause 6 represents one of the steps to that end' (cited in Saville
1986, p.298).

   Another step to the same end was the Government's abolition
of the Fair Wages Resolution, which hitherto had obliged
government contractors to adhere to at least minimum rates of pay
and working conditions. Instead of using its powers to encourage
generous treatment of workers in firms contracted to it, the
Government used them to encourage the creation of a low wage
economy. Public authorities were increasingly obliged to put their
services out to tender, and were instructed to take the cheapest
tender without regard to the terms and conditions of employment
on offer by the company concerned. The contracting-out of public
services to private firms then both encouraged and legitimised 'the
most blatant form of wage cutting' since 'in numerous cases the
same workers (were) rehired by the sub-contracting firm with
reduced pay and benefits, more intensive workloads and sometimes
on an explicitly non-union basis: all under the guise of greater
efficiency' (Longstreth 1988, p.6). This privatisation of public
services positively invited wage cutting, as firms struggled to
undercut each other's tenders; and the result was that employment
shifted to non-unionised, part-time, often female and young male

workers, with only the minimum access to sick pay, holidays and pensions won by better organised workers in easier times.

One other element in the Thatcherite strategy to shift class power was the toleration of the end of these 'easier times'. By keeping a tight control on the money supply in its first term of office, by cutting subsidies to private firms, and by allowing capital to be exported without controls, the Conservative Government after 1979 engineered the severest recession ever experienced by British industry, and tolerated an unprecedented growth in the scale of unemployment. 'The collapse in output and employment was the worst ever, outstripping that of 1920–22, and far worse than that of the 1930s. Between 1929 and 1931, 0.8 million jobs were lost, but by 1936 over 2.5 million new jobs had been created and manufacturing output was one-third higher than its 1929 level' (MacInnes 1987, p.67). Under the Thatcher Government, by contrast, between December 1979 and December 1982 employment in manufacturing fell by a staggering 21%. 1.5 million jobs were lost in the manufacturing sector as total unemployment rose from 1.2 million in June 1979 to 2.9 million in June 1983. Another 300,000 jobs were then lost in manufacturing from March 1983 to September 1986, and though these were compensated to a degree by a growth of employment in services and among the self-employed, even on the 'laundered' statistics issued by the Government (which changed the way it counted the unemployed no less than 19 times in its first 8 years in office, to take probably 500,000 people 'out' of the figures) unemployment still rose to 3.3 million by September 1985, and had only slipped back to 2,375,000 by the middle of 1988. As Theo Nichols observed:

> Market forces have bitten all right, and British manufacturing workforces have been very substantially 'slimmed'. Between 1977 and 1983, for example, employment fell by between 25 and 30 per cent at British Shipbuilders and Lucas, by over 30 per cent at Vauxhall, ICI and Massey Ferguson, by 50 per cent or more at Courtaulds, BL, GKN, Tube Investments and Dunlop, and by over 60 per cent at British Steel and Talbot . . . A whole mass of less well known medium and small firms collapsed entirely.
>
> (Nichols 1987, pp.206–7)

The full figures on unemployment to its peak in 1985 are given in Table 5.1.

Table 5.1   Unemployment 1978–85

1978	1,343,000
1979	1,234,000
1980	1,513,000
1981	2,395,000
1982	2,770,000
1983	2,984,000
1984	3,284,000
1985	3,346,000

Source: Key Data, 1986 (CSO 1986, London) p.14
Note: The figures for 1984 and 1985 are for September. Earlier figures are annual
averages.

The Conservative Government orchestrated a hostile public opinion, introduced new legal barriers, and tolerated large-scale unemployment to erode the power of organised labour; and it also used its own role as employer and as financier of the unemployed to the same end. It actually banned trade unions from GCHQ; and refused to accept unions there even in return for a no-disruption pledge. It intervened more and more in the area of youth employment, setting rates of pay—through its Youth Training Schemes—which had a depressive effect on unskilled and youth wages generally. As we will see in detail in a moment, it encouraged anti-union policies from its senior managerial figures in the manufacturing parts of the public sector (particularly from Sir Michael Edwardes, already in place at British Leyland, and from Ian MacGregor, brought in at great expense first at British Steel, then at the National Coal Board); and it subjected its own civil servants to intensified managerial policies which were superintended by senior figures seconded from the private sector. The Thatcher Government regularly and repeatedly imposed tight cash limits on all government departments and public bodies, and so in effect ran its own incomes policy in the public sector—trading wages for jobs, and whittling away the size of both. It even, in the case of the teachers, totally abandoned existing collective bargaining machinery—and imposed its own settlement—in spite of a prolonged industrial struggle by the teaching unions concerned.

So this Government did not leave private employers or market forces to bear the brunt of the attack on trade union power. It encouraged the private sector to assert its right to manage, and it orchestrated market forces to that end. But it also took its own unions on—one by one—when it was ready. It led the attack on trade union power from the front, by example, and did so with some enthusiasm. For the Thatcher Government not only set out to shift class power decisively. It also set out to break the power of public sector unionism. It had its own private account to settle, particularly with the National Union of Mineworkers; and in the settling of that account, more than any other, it was prepared to tolerate prolonged industrial disruption and the expenditure of quite vast sums of public money.

II

John Saville has referred to the Conservative Government's handling of the miners' dispute of 1984–5 as an 'open conspiracy' (Saville 1986, p.295); and indeed it was. The roots of that conspiracy run back to at least 1978, when the Conservative Party received two internal reports on the power of unionism in the public sector. By then the 'defeat' of the Heath Government by the miners in 1972 and 1973–4 had entered the folklore of British politics; and had left throughout the Conservative Party deep concern with, and apprehension about, future trade union policy. The images of 1972 remained potent: particularly those of 10,000 engineering workers marching out of Birmingham behind their union banners to help flying pickets from the Yorkshire coalfields close the Saltley Coke Works in February 1972—in what must surely be one of the most dramatic demonstrations of working class industrial power and solidarity witnessed in Britain since 1926 (see Geary 1986, p.76). That of course was not the only image of picketing which persisted from 1972. Equally potent was that 'of a lone NUM picket holding a placard at a railway bridge: a symbolic barrier which the drivers on the line below refused to cross' (Hyman 1986, p.335). Those events and memories had created— in one wing of the Conservative Party—the firm belief that 'strong unions, and the advanced technology operated by their members, particularly in fuel and power industries, mean that no government these days can "win" in the way Mr. Baldwin's Cabinet triumphed during the General Strike of 1926 by maintaining essential supplies and services' (the Carrington Report to Mrs. Thatcher, cited in *The Times*, 18.4.1978, p.1). But more resilient voices within the Thatcher party were less sure. They argued instead that a quite different lesson ought to be drawn from the experience of the Heath Government: namely that the defeat of trade union power would not be easy, but it was still vital and so would have to be *carefully planned*.

So in the same year as Lord Carrington's Report, 1978, *The Economist* was able to leak details of an internal party document drawn up by Nicholas Ridley—the so-called 'Ridley Plan'—which took a distinctly more aggressive attitude to the question of trade union power. In his report, Nicholas Ridley distinguished industries in which the Government could be effectively blackmailed by trade union power from those in which it could not: listing as the Government's vulnerable spots sewerage, water, electricity, gas and the health service; as its least vulnerable, ports, telephones, air transport and steel; and as intermediately vulnerable, railways, docks, coal, and refuse removal. The Report recommended concessions in the vulnerable industries and the preparation of an effective strategy to defeat union challenges in the rest. Ridley argued that, long before a major dispute loomed, a Conservative Government should:

rig the return on capital to allow above-norm pay settlements in 'vulnerable' sectors, especially electricity and gas;

pick the battleground where and when it could win (Ridley mentioned coal, the railways, British Leyland, the civil service and steel); and in the event of an impending coal strike in particular:
— build up coal stocks and delay confrontation until these were in place;
— make contingency plans for the import of coal;
— encourage the recruitment of non-union lorry drivers in the haulage companies to help move coal during the strike;
— cut social security payments to strikers, to make the union finance them;
— prepare a large mobile squad of police to uphold the law against violent picketing.

That Report prefigured with quite remarkable accuracy many of the unusual features of the miners' strike of 1984–5. The strike came at the end of a long series of industrial disputes in the public sector which the Government and management had ridden out and won; and came only after police tactics to break mass picketing had been practiced successfully in the NGA dispute with Eddie Shah at Warrington. The strike occurred three years after the Conservative Government had 'ducked' NUM militancy over NCB plans to cut the number of pits and miners. As the Secretary of State for Energy at the time, David Howell, admitted later: 'neither the Government nor I think society as a whole was in a position to get locked into a coal strike . . . in those days stocks weren't so high. I don't think the country was prepared, and the whole NUM and trade union movement tended to be united on one side' (cited in Saville 1986, p.304). So in 1981 the Conservatives avoided confrontation; and waited until 1984, when coal stocks were high, the police and road haulage companies were ready, and when the management style of Ian MacGregor had been transferred from British Steel to the NCB. By then, too, as we saw earlier, changes had been made to social security legislation, to leave the burden of sustaining striking miners through a long dispute fully on the shoulders of the union and its supporters.

The strike was provoked by the decision to close down the pit at Cortonwood in the spring of 1984: summer was coming, coal stocks were at an all-time high, and the trade unions were already reeling from the effects of mass unemployment, hostile legislation and big defeats at British Leyland and British Steel. The strike lasted 51 weeks, from March 1984 to February 1985; and its length reflected the degree to which the Government steadfastly refused to co-operate with the repeated attempts of church leaders and others to mediate a compromise settlement which would allow the NUM to withdraw without loss of face. Instead of compromise, the Government organised for total success, and deployed its vast resources to achieve it. Throughout the strike, the Home Secretary superintended the use of up to 20,000 police men and women in a nationally co-ordinated operation that involved major confrontations between mass ranks of police officers and pickets, and the systematic closing off of entry to strike-bound areas. NUM sympathisers were stopped from entering Nottinghamshire—the focus of the dispute—from as far away as the Dartford tunnel in Kent; and 'the Chief Constable of Nottinghamshire estimated that 164,508 individuals, presumed pickets, were stopped from entering the county in the first 27 weeks of the strike' (McIlroy 1985a, pp.106–7) alone. Having been severely criticised by Margaret Thatcher early in the strike for allowing mass picketing, the police responded by deploying initially in Nottingham '1,000 police, within days 8,000, and after the first week over 20,000 officers . . . The police were determined to match and outnumber the pickets. As early as March 21' they 'reported a ratio of almost 8:1' and 'this degree of commitment continued throughout the dispute. It was graphically highlighted at Cortonwood in the autumn when fifteen hundred police stood to escort one miner to work' (ibid., p.106).

Not surprisingly with such a police presence, pickets were arrested in large numbers: more than 9,000 in 1984 alone. They were then often charged with serious offences, and bailed only on conditions that barred them from returning to picket duty; and in this way the 'flying picket' tactic of 1972 was harassed and minimised into ineffectiveness. And if that was not enough, phones were tapped and legal injunctions served, to undermine union power still further. In the event, the new employment legislation was not used. Instead, the Government and the NCB left it to individual union members to challenge NUM picketing under *civil law*; and this proved to be sufficiently potent a legal device to allow the State 'to sequester the NUM's assets and drive it down to defeat, not ostensibly in the interests of government and employer but to protect the unions' own members' (McIlroy 1985a, p.116). This legal dimension proved in the end crucial to the NUM's failure;* and by the end of the strike, the leaders of the Kent miners had spent ten days in jail, the national leadership had been fined for contempt, and the assets of the national union had been totally sequestered and placed under the control of a Tory councillor for North Derbyshire.

Of course, the judiciary, the police and the law were not the main barriers to winning the miners' strike. 'All the police and

---

* This need not surprise us. As Richard Hyman has recently observed, 'the archaic principles of common law embody an overriding commitment to the rights of property and the sanctity of individual contracts; and this bias is reinforced by the trained prejudices of the judges whose powers enable them to act, in effect, as surrogate legislators. In consequence, British law contains a built-in presumption that trade unions, strikes, and all other collective efforts by workers to offset their individual weakness in the face of the employer, are illegal conspiracies "in restraint of trade"' (Hyman 1987, p.94).

legal judgements in the world could not have kept the Nottinghamshire pits working, the steel industry operating, and the power stations functioning, if the workers in them had laid down their tools and supported the miners' (McIlroy 1985a, p.121). But this time they did not. Right-wing trade union leadership among electricians and steel workers, the generalised fear of unemployment, a hostile judiciary and a series of previous defeats at the hands of the Conservatives, kept most workers away from the miners' dispute, prepared to give food, money, but not sympathy action. In fact the strike had been irreparably damaged from the outset both by the refusal of Nottinghamshire miners to obey the strike call and by the NUM leadership's decision not to ballot. But support groups did flourish, and kept a flow of money, food and people moving into the coalfields throughout the strike and in spite of the police; and in this way made a significant contribution to the strike's longevity.

No such contribution, however, was forthcoming from either the TUC or the national leadership of the Labour Party. From them, the NUM attracted only vestigial support of a token kind (of statements, token presence on picket lines, and parliamentary pressure for concessions from the Government). But that was all. 'The TUC in September 1984 declared its "total support" for the NUM in its dispute, but whatever the rhetoric, its leaders took care not to come into conflict with the law' (Hyman 1987, p.98). Likewise, the Labour Party Shadow Cabinet under Neil Kinnock declined to back the strike unambiguously, apparently more afraid of the electoral consequences in marginal constituencies of the strike's success than of the general demoralisation likely to come with its defeat. As John Saville said:

> The conduct of the Parliamentary Labour Party during the miners' strike can only be described as unprincipled, and lacking, not only in integrity, but in plain commonsense. The strike was a provocation; that was widely said in the Commons by speakers from the Labour side; and it lasted a year. The Labour Party in Parliament were given the opportunity to begin a serious educational campaign to explain the politics of Thatcherism in the context of the miners' strike. Of course to do this they needed a comprehensive energy policy, which they had not got; they would be required to understand how the NCB and the Government were falsifying the annual accounts of the coal industry, and this was not appreciated because someone or some group within the Labour Party apparatus

had not recognised the problem; and third, it would have required
political courage to withstand the lying propaganda of most of the
media, and the Labour Party leadership was regrettably short of
courage.   (Saville 1986, p.326)

So there was no co-ordinated national Labour Party policy to
'initiate action in support of the miners' cause, to point vigorously
to questions of unemployment and energy policy, to raise clearly
important issues about civil rights and the workings of the police
force and the legal system' (Beynon 1985, p.22); and because there
was not, the Labour leadership itself helped to create the
conditions in which eventually the miners were forced into defeat.
For in the end—and in spite of the dignity with which striking
miners marched back into their pits behind their union banners—
the strike was defeated; and it was followed (as broken strikes
often are) by the systematic victimisation of militants, the
weakening of the Left within the union, and the breakaway of a
separate and right-wing union organisation (in this case, the Union
of Democratic Mineworkers).

We must realise too that these subsequent developments within
the coal industry and the NUM were just the most immediate and
localised consequences of a struggle that the Conservative
Government had long recognised to be of immense importance to
its general and underlying goal: of ending, once and for all, the
power of organised labour in British society, and thereby eroding
the basis for any electoral revival by the Labour Party. The
Conservative Government under Margaret Thatcher had no doubt
that breaking union power was the key to the success of its general
economic strategy: that 'unless the ball and chain, the irons and
handcuffs of traditional trade union attitudes are struck off, we
will continue to be handicapped in the race for markets,
customers, orders and jobs' (Tebbitt, cited in Mitchell 1987a,
p.34). One of his colleagues even went so far as to claim, in 1985,
that 'in the context of a thousand years of British history their
taming of the unions will be seen as a significant event beyond
calculation' (ibid., p.33); and if that claim was wildly overdrawn,
the fact that it could be made at all indicated the strategic vision
underlying Conservative policy to the unions throughout the
1980s.

Certainly, this strategic sense informed the Conservative
Government's resilience throughout the miners' strike, and kept it

in the forefront of the battle to defeat Arthur Scargill and his colleagues. At the same time, and by the same token, the parallel absence of such a strategic sense in Labour's leadership had the reverse effect, setting the Labour Party on the sidelines, unable and unwilling at national level to match Tory resilience with an equivalent counter-resistance of its own. No Labour leader outside the Labour Left was willing to match the Conservative class perspectives of a Norman Tebbitt with class perspectives of a socialist kind. Tebbitt was quite prepared to argue in public that only a defeat of the NUM could significantly reduce the likelihood of further major national stoppages and enhance the prospect of unbroken Tory rule in the 1990s. For that was how much was at stake in the miners' strike of 1984–5, and the Tories knew it. The tragedy for left-wing forces in this country is that, apparently, the Labour leadership did not.

III

When Mrs Thatcher celebrated on the day that her tenure of office became longer than any previous Prime Minister this century, she told the Press Association that her Government had 'cured Britain of a sickness' by replacing the 'British disease' with 'a lot more harmony in industry'. 'We have brought', she said,

> to the acknowledgement of the world, a more confident and a more prosperous Britain. They used, when I first came in, to talk about us in terms of the British disease. Now they talk about us and say 'Look, Britain has got the cure. Come to Britain to see how Britain has done it'. That is an enormous turnround. And it has brought hope to others as well. (*Guardian*, 4.1.1988, p.3)

There is no doubt that this is how the Thatcher Government understands its own achievement, and how its impact has been read by many both here and abroad. Yet, in spite of so consistently held an impression, it is actually very difficult to isolate with any precision the contribution of Thatcherism to the shaping of industrial relations in contemporary Britain. The processes we need to measure are still in train. The forces that shape them are many and complex; and initiatives are easier to isolate than are the consequences to which they give rise. And yet what evidence we have would suggest that—in spite of the claims made for it both by its admirers and its critics—the impact of this Government on the crucial area of capital–labour relations has not been as great as the politicians expected; and that the further you move from those areas of industrial relations directly controlled by the State, the more limited the impact becomes.

Industrial relations in contemporary Britain are shaped by more than directly political forces. Long-term secular trends shape industrial relations too—those which derive from the organisation of capital and from the competition between and within classes. The Thatcher initiatives have accentuated some of these, and fallen victim to others. The Thatcherite concern, for example, to *shift employment* away from traditional union strongholds in private manufacturing and public sector employment towards largely unorganised private services has had a mixed pattern of success. The Conservatives have not managed to cut the percentage of civilian employees in the public sector by more than 5%, and 'if the public sector corporations are excluded where privatisation reduced the number of public employees dramatically by transferring them to the private sector, then the proportion of public employees actually increased, because of the fall of employment in private industry' (MacInnes 1987, p.77). It is true that the government-induced recession brought a significant rise in the scale of job losses in the manufacturing sector; but those job losses began long before 1979, and the recession cut jobs in services too. As late as 1985 the Conservatives had still failed to preside over as large an expansion in service employment as did the Labour Government between 1974 and 1979.

The resulting impact of Thatcherite policies on patterns of *trade union growth* is equally complex. In the 1980s the steady upward growth of union membership under Labour has been reversed. After rising by 3 million in a decade to peak at 13.3 million members in 1979, the trade union movement lost 2.5 million of that total by 1985. Yet as Table 5.2 shows, the worst of that loss occurred early—nearly 2 million had gone by 1982—and the absolute decline has slowed down significantly since. The scale of loss, though of course very serious for the unions involved, is still modest when compared with the 50% collapse in union member-

Table 5.2 Union Membership and Density in the United Kingdom, Selected Years

	Union membership	Union membership as % of potential membership
1978	13,112,000	54.4
1979	13,298,000	54.6
1980	12,927,000	52.9
1981	12,106,000	49.9
1982	11,593,000	47.8
1983	11,236,000	46.8
1984	10,994,000	45.4
1985	10,716,000	43.5

Source: Longstreth (1988).

ship figures in the inter-war depression; and it is almost entirely to be explained by the loss of *jobs* by union members, and not by any withdrawal from unionism by people still in work. In fact, under Thatcher 'the proportions of establishments recognising unions has actually risen in the service sector (41% in 1980 to 44% in 1984) and in the public one (94% to 99%); and has fallen in manufacturing (65% to 56%) only because of the disproportionate rate of closure of large manufacturing plants which tend to be highly unionised' (Longstreth 1988, p.10). The restructuring of employment away to professional and financial services, and to high-tech green-field-based industries—in all of which trade unionism is traditionally weak—has had an impact, keeping the density of union membership low (at 21%) among private firms expanding their employment most. 'Whatever happens to aggregate employment in the rest of the 1980s . . . its structural composition will almost inevitably continue to move away from concentrated workplaces in the large industrial centres to smaller and more displaced workplaces and to the private service sector which has traditionally proved resistant to unionism' (Hyman 1987, p.116). To this degree at least, therefore, structural changes in employment, rather than Thatcherism, may be succeeding in *containing* trade unionism to areas it has already colonised; but nonetheless, in spite of all the unemployment and the new legislation, what evidence we have still suggests that 'formal union organisation has not been seriously eroded in those sectors in which it was previously well-established' (ibid., p.10). In fact, in the economy as a whole, nearly one worker in two was still a union member in 1985.

The style of *assertive management* encouraged by the Conservative Government during the miners' strike was successfully deployed in all the major public sector disputes of the early Thatcher years. In all of those (among steelworkers, health service workers, railway drivers and teachers) strikers eventually returned to work on terms that were not significantly better than those offered to them at the start of the dispute. And this success encouraged many other employers in the private sector to follow suit. Indeed, 'macho management' as it was popularly known 'became a widespread feature of British industrial relations: an aggressive insistence on "management's right to manage", a sharp reduction in the area of the negotiable' (Hyman 1988, p.170). It has been particularly visible in the newspaper industry, where private employers (first Times newspapers, then Eddie Shah, and latterly Rupert Murdoch) have used the tighter laws on picketing to attack successfully the control of the production process exercised by the print unions. In the latter two of those three examples, resistance by the workers affected still brought mass picketing, and violent clashes between strikers and police on the streets of Warrington and Wapping; and this drew from the State the same reaction as had picketing by the miners—namely, injunctions before the courts, sequestration of assets, and the deployment of enormous numbers of police officers whose presence was enough, in the end, to give the employer total victory (though with Rupert Murdoch at Wapping, victory came too only with the connivance of the electricians union, and in all cases—as with the miners—because of the refusal or inability of the TUC to mobilise wider working class support).

That style of management also surfaced in the manufacturing part of the public sector, in cars and in steel, where demand had long exceeded supply, and where 'ironically, the fact that these companies are state-owned has probably encouraged a hard-line strategy, in order to win continued financial backing from the Thatcher Government' (Hyman 1988, p.171). Michael Edwardes at British Leyland fired Derek Robinson, the senior convenor, in

1979, saw industrial resistance to that sacking peter out, and then introduced new procedures and working practices which marginalised shop stewards and returned significant degrees of control over production back to line management (Willman 1984, p.8). The Edwardes strategy constituted 'a combined attack on shopfloor organisation, by reducing the numbers of full-time shop stewards and restricting the mobility of others, by attempts to "by pass" them by obtaining workplace opinion directly through ballots and referenda, and by the unilateral imposition of sets of working arrangements designed to reduce or eliminate "restrictive practices"' (Terry 1983, p.90). British Leyland then used its new managerial power to intensify the work process—'to remove those barriers to productivity increases which lay in inefficient use of labour or interruptions to its supply' (Willman 1984, p.9)—and to push through low pay deals. Ian MacGregor did a not dissimilar job at British Steel. After successfully weathering what was, in 1980, the longest national dispute since the war, British Steel's management shut plants, fired militants, and intensified working practices, with the unions too weak and exhausted to offer any more resistance: so that in the case of British Steel, the workforce was reduced in size by nearly two-thirds from 1980 to 1986, and the industry was prepared for privatisation.

But such direct attacks on trade union power at local level were very much the minority response among private employers: outside the print industry (where the print unions had established a particularly strong hold on the work process because of the uniquely perishable character of the commodity they produced) anti-unionism was more likely to be found among small and new employers than among large and established ones. 'The majority of established employers have not adopted such tough tactics, but have (instead) exploited the weakening of trade union bargaining power within a framework of continued trade union rights' (Terry 1983, p.90). 'For the most part employers did not rush in to wield the powers provided for them' (Taylor 1987b, p.23) by the new trade union legislation. Many personnel directors in large firms remained well aware of the importance of good labour relations, and of the contribution to them which can be made by recognised trade union officials and long-established negotiating procedures. So in firms such as these, workers did not find themselves facing an anti-union employer.

Instead, workers found themselves facing employers owning many plants, employers whose experience of intensifying competition left them progressively less able to tolerate low levels of managerial control over detailed working practices and over locally-negotiated rates of pay. In those firms, personnel management became increasingly sophisticated and extensive through the 1970s and 1980s. Work study techniques were used more frequently, even before the return of the Thatcher Government. 'The Warwick survey suggests that their use . . . increased in a third of manufacturing establishments with over 50 employees over the years 1973–8' (Purcell and Sissons 1983, p.104); and companies began to insist on company-wide and highly detailed collective agreements. To obtain these, 'to restrict the scope of collective bargaining and avoiding it altogether, if possible, at the point of production' (ibid., p.103), and to make such agreements stick, managements were positively keen to deal directly with at least senior shop stewards; and the stewards found themselves to be the recipients of offices, telephones, and regular access to personnel management.

This was not the Edwardes strategy. The power of shop stewards was not to be broken by direct confrontation, or by-passed by direct appeals to workers, as at British Leyland. Instead, the power of shop stewards was *co-opted* to a joint venture sold to workers through sophisticated communications, underpinned by fear of job loss, and negotiated into place in deals struck with shopfloor representatives. What this managerial response constituted was an attempt 'not to destroy shop steward organisation, but rather to "mould" it into a particular form, intentionally or not, (combining) to exaggerate certain tendencies, present in the earlier shop steward model, towards centralisation, formalisation, and professionalisation of shop stewards and their organisations' (Terry 1983, p.85). Richard Hyman has described the overall situation in these terms:

> 'Macho management' characterized by the total repudiation of trade unionism is not yet typical of British employers. Three tendencies are, however, widespread. The first is a far greater sophistication than in the past. Large multi-plant (and often transnational) firms pursue centrally co-ordinated objectives, often in the face of union organisation still committed to the autonomy of each workplace; the issues on which to risk or even provoke confrontation are often carefully chosen. Secondly, the area of the

negotiable has been sharply restricted; managements increasingly insist on their 'right to manage', merely offering to 'consult' with union representatives over production-related issues. Third, piece-meal encroachments have been made on rights of collective organisation: notably, in many companies, a cutback in shop steward facilities. Often this is associated with the cultivation of alternative channels of management–worker relations: various forms of 'joint participation' at workplace level, and in some cases Japanese-style 'quality circles' designed to strengthen workers' commitment to the company's production goals.

(Hyman 1985, pp.116–7)

What the Thatcher Government then did was not to block this strategy, but to create market conditions in which it could yield more to the managements who used it: by reducing the degree of worker resistance to the introduction of new techniques, of tighter management, and of greater flexibility of labour. All that, however, was squeezed out of workers in the Thatcher years from collective bargaining institutions which had already eroded shop floor power *before* the Thatcher Government came to office. As William Brown reported in his 1978 survey of manufacturing industry:

Ten years before our survey, industrial relations in manufacturing was dominated by multi-employer agreements . . . By 1978 that had been transformed. For two-thirds of manual and three-quarters of non-manual employees, the formal structure of bargaining has become one of single-employer agreements covering one or more factories within a company. Multi-employer agreements have not vanished. They are still adhered to in many factories with small workforces, and in industries such as clothing and printing which have a large number of small companies, but they cover only a quarter of the manual and a tenth of the non-manual manufacturing force. (Brown 1981, p.118)

Brown and his colleagues found that pay in these company-wide agreements was 'increasingly fixed by a single bargaining unit, rather than added to on successive bargaining levels'. They also found that this meant that pay was settled further away from the shop floor than in the 1950s and 1960s, and that in the process the shop stewards had moved to centre-stage. 'Particularly in larger establishments,' he wrote, 'stewards now have complex organis-ations and strong procedural recognition'—and this change had become especially 'noticeable among non-manual workers in industries where, a decade ago, there was little workplace bargaining' (ibid., p.119)

By bringing decision making on industrial relations down from national to company level, and up from shop floor to board room, the trend among larger firms in British manufacturing industry to company-wide agreements has changed the role, but not undermined the existence, of the shop steward whose power has been a target of government policy since the early 1960s. For there were quite simply not enough full-time trade union officials to carry the workload of negotiation at company level; and personnel directors were left with little choice but to negotiate, in the main, with convenors, senior stewards, lay branch secretaries and other lay union officers on the company payroll. In the mid-1960s it was estimated that such senior stewards were probably outnumbered by full-time officials in some ratio of 2:3. As early as the mid-1970s, however, all the evidence suggests that the relationship in size between the two groups had been reversed (Boraston *et al.* 1975, p.193); and as late as 1984, the survey of British workplace industrial relations found: 'in the private sector, (and) controlling for the size of the manual workforce, there was an indication that senior stewards were becoming more common rather than less' (Millward and Stevens 1985, p.82).

Not all shop stewards are, or were, equally powerful, of course. On the contrary: 'a central feature of the past ten years has been the consolidation of a *hierarchy* within shop steward organisation' (Hyman 1988, p.6) such that 'in many of the newer schemes the majority of shop stewards have little direct role in wage determination which is handled by a negotiating committee, or even by one person' (Terry 1983, p.80). What has emerged in fact is 'a substantial stratum of (more or less) full-time senior shop stewards, wielding considerable power within their workplace organisations, and performing a key mediating role between employers, union officials and the ordinary membership (including "first line" shop stewards)' (Hyman 1980, p.74). Within the procedural changes introduced into industrial relations in the manufacturing sector *before* the arrival of Thatcherism, we can see the bureaucratisation and centralisation of shop steward organisation, and the encouragement by management of independent stewards organisations capable of operating without full-time officials, and at a distance from the memberships from which originally they sprang. In other words, and quite independently of Thatcherite enthusiasm for Japanese-style management, large firms in British manufacturing had already begun to decentralise their collective bargaining back to company level, and were encouraging developments in shop steward organisation that could herald the creation of 'company unions'. Even before the arrival of Thatcherite labour law, powerful processes were at work within British industry to weaken that link between shop stewards and their members which had produced, in the twenty years before, a significant degree of working class control at the point of production.

When the Brown survey of 1978 was replicated and extended in the early and mid-1980s, it emerged that little had changed during the early Thatcher years. Union recognition remained extensive, collective bargaining for pay was stable everywhere except in manufacturing (where, as we have already noted, its percentage fall was entirely due to the closure of plants with collective bargaining machinery), and the system of shop stewards remained firmly intact. Indeed, the number of stewards actually increased between 1980 and 1984, in spite of the fall in total employment. Millward and Stevens estimate that the total number of stewards rose by 6% between 1980 and 1984—from 317,000 to 335,000; and that their distribution by employment sector changed even more markedly. They record a 27% drop in the number of stewards in manufacturing, an 18% rise in services, and a 31% rise in the number of stewards in the public sector (Millward and Stevens 1985, p.85). Overall by 1984 'there were almost as many white collar stewards as manual ones' (MacInnes 1987 p.100).

So, 'when we consider the impact of economic restructuring, the results suggest that workplace trade unionism did rather well' under Thatcher. 'The unions appear to be increasing their organisation in areas of the economy in which they had been weaker such as private services and white collar jobs, and which were the expanding areas of the economy' (ibid., p.100). Where unions were not strong, and where they remain weak, is in the small business sector. There, in workplaces with less than 25 employees, union density is probably no greater than 27% (ibid., p.101). The number of workers in closed shops also appears to be falling: from 5.2 million in 1978 to perhaps less than 4 million by 1984: and certainly 'there have been no significant new closed shops established since 1980' (Mitchell 1987a, p.40). Yet even this was 'largely due to the contraction of the docks industry and printing where closed shops used to predominate (Taylor 1987b, p.22), rather than to legislative changes, however draconian. It would therefore be a mistake to see even low levels of unionisation in small firms, or shrinkages in the scale of the closed shop, as unambiguous evidence of a renewed employers' offensive to roll back trade unionism. As ACAS reported on the Thatcher years in 1986:

> Cases in which companies withdrew negotiating or consultative rights remained very much the exception. Overall, where union membership was well-established, it remained so, and collective bargaining and consultative machinery continued to be the major means through which employers and employees dealt with each other.   (cited in Taylor 1987b, p.22)

In spite of government rhetoric and tough labour laws, therefore, it would seem that the basic institutions of workplace trade unionism remain strong; and that thus far at least the impact of Thatcherism on negotiating structures has been only limited and marginal. Table 5.3 gives trade union density in British manufacturing and service industries after the first five years of the Thatcher attack on trade union power.

Table 5.3   Trade Union Density in Manufacturing and Service Industries, 1984 (%)

	Manufacturing	*Services*
Average density: all workers	58	58
Average density: manual workers	72	63
Average density: non-manual workers	35	55

Source: Millward and Stevens (1985) pp. 55 and 56.

The impact of Thatcherism has been far greater, of course, on what came out of those negotiating structures than on the workings of the structures themselves. Procedures could stay intact because the weakened position of labour undermined the capacity of workers to use them to block managerial change. As Sir Donald Wass, former head of the Treasury, put it, 'what has emerged in shop floor behaviour through fear and anxiety is much greater than I think could be secured by more co-operative methods' (quoted in Nichols 1987, p.176). Undeniably, there has been an employers' offensive of a particular kind in the 1980s, against working class power in industry. 'Commercial pressures, and the changed balance of labour power have brought the unilateral imposition of re-organisation and speed up, regardless of union (and especially shop steward) resistance. The threat of closure has itself provided a potent sanction: workers have been offered the stark choice of co-operating with management or losing their jobs' (Hyman 1985, p.116). There is evidence that this new-found managerial power has been used widely in British manufacturing industry in recent years. 'For example, over 80% of manufacturing plants surveyed in 1984 had introduced changes in the previous two years, and over 50% of those plants had introduced three or more changes' (Rubery 1986, p.96). These changes 'often involved a higher intensity of labour effort and the introduction of more flexible forms of working, which in a majority of cases also meant the relaxation of well-established demarcation lines' (ibid.). Apparently, and so far, the bulk of this additional flexibility has occurred within, and not between, grades and so has not yet led either to the 'widespread deskilling and downgrading of labour' or to a systematic erosion of craft differentials (though significantly Vauxhall tried that in its pay proposals to its skilled and semi-skilled labour force in 1987). But even so it is clear that 'the threat of closure has . . . provided employers with a powerful sanction in forcing through reorganis-ation and speed up in the face of union (and particularly shop steward) resistance', and that 'poor productivity and declining competitiveness have encouraged manufacturing firms to pursue radical programmes of rationalisation, involving more flexible use of labour, more intensive working, tighter disciplinary regulations, and hence a systematic assault on established custom and practice' (Hyman 1988, p.171). Though its precise impact is hard to isolate, there can be no doubt that this 'offensive' made a significant contribution to the 21% increase in manufacturing productivity achieved across British industry as a whole between 1982 and 1986, and it certainly constituted the successful diminution in shop steward and work group power which corporatist administrations had sought in vain before 1979.

IV

What seems to be emerging under Thatcherism in Britain is some kind of dual labour market economy. At its core are well-organised, unionised, and relatively protected white male full-time workers, surrounded by a secondary circle of the less well-paid, less unionised and less secure workers: often part-time, commonly female, and young, and black. Those in the core enjoy a high degree of job security and tolerable working conditions, while more peripheral workers experience poorer conditions, 'more directly determined by the market and with security of employment dependent on how busy the firm is' (MacInnes 1987, p.113). The division between types of worker is well illustrated in Figure 5.1.

This division between core and periphery workers has contradictory effects on the well-organised workers at the centre. It has

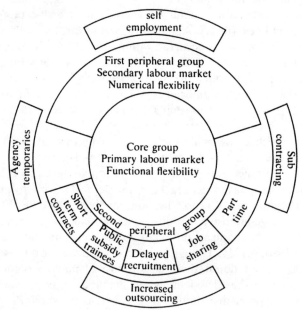

Source: Nichols (1987), p.202: from Atkinson (1984), p.29.

Figure 5.1 The Flexible Firm

left them the negotiating power to keep their wage rates ahead of inflation, as we will see; but it has also obliged them to negotiate in a more competitive climate, one in which the risk of exclusion from the core is ever present. To protect their jobs, workers in the core, with greater or lesser degrees of resistance depending on local market factors, have tolerated a diminution in their degree of job control, an intensification of their work routines, and the erosion of established working practices. For the threat of reclassification—out of the core and into the unemployed—is always around them. So too, depending on how easily their skills can be replaced, is the threat of reclassification into, or more probably replacement by, the growing army of the part-time, the young, and contract workers.

It does look as though, in ways comparable to the more common practice in Japan, firms here in the 1980s tried to protect their core of skilled and dependable labour by subcontracting to specialist suppliers and to self-employed workers, and by employing temporary workers on limited contracts, and people on government training schemes. Such reliance on cheap and temporary labour, non-unionised and with limited employee rights, has long been common in some industries—in hotels and catering, for example—where the pressure to keep wage costs down is particularly high; and 'there is growing evidence that employers outside the service sector are (also) moving towards a system of "segmented workforces of fixed and variable components", through the use of marginal employment forms, although so far this is less part of their long term planning than an immediate response to conditions of uncertainty and the need to cut labour costs' (Deakin 1986, p.228). The Government's contribution here has been indirect but crucial. Government policy on the privatisation of public services has encouraged such hiring practices, as has its repeal of the fair wages resolution. For in the wake of these changes of policy, 'the extent of sub-contracting within the public sector generally has grown', so 'detaching part of the workforce from the main body: the typical result is a lowering of wage levels and a reduction in fringe benefits such as sick pay, and in the level of job security' (Deakin 1986, p.228).

More generally, the restructuring of labour law has encouraged the spread of low-paid, part-time work. Even the Labour Government's employment protection legislation was dualist in nature, providing thresholds below which part-time work was less hedged about with workers' rights and employers' obligations; and in fact 'the number of part-time jobs increased between 1971 and 1981 by over one million, an increase of 34%' (Beechey and Perkins 1987, p.30). 'Changes in the legislative schemes since 1979 have exacerbated the position of marginal workers, by extending the qualifying period for unfair dismissal, and by providing for contracting out in fixed term contracts of one year or more in length' (Deakin 1986, p.239). Part-time work is particularly endemic in the service sector, and its growth in total (it increased by 340,000 between 1981 and 1987, as full-time employment fell by 1 million) is in large measure to be explained by the growth of the service sector.

Overall, 'the trends of the 1970s have been continued into the 1980s, with a further 579,000 part-time jobs for women being created between December 1981 and December 1985. At present just over five million jobs are done by part-time women workers, and nearly half of all women's jobs are part-time' (Beechey and Perkins 1987, p.37). In fact, 'about one in five employees in Britain—that is, nearly 4 million people—work part-time' (Schoer 1987, p.83) 'and the overwhelming percentage of these are women.' 'The United Kingdom has the highest proportion of women part-time workers of any OECD country. . . . According to the 1981 census, over 90% of part-time workers were women, and 87% of these were married' (Beechey and Perkins 1987, pp.16–17). 'At least half a million people additionally work as temps, on contract, freelance, or as homeworkers, and in this category too high percentages of the workers involved are women' (Deakin 1986, p.228). In addition, young workers, and black workers of every age and gender, are disproportionately represented in these non-core areas of employment; and of course, as a result, in the ranks of the unemployed as well.

Government involvement has been more direct in the organisation of youth employment, in the funding of the long-term unemployed, and in the maintenance of other groups of workers unable to sell their labour power because of disability, domestic responsibilities, or age. The consistent thrust of legislative change here has been to encourage people to move off benefit and into low-paid unskilled labour. Consistent with its commitment to a market economy, the Thatcher Government has sought systematically to weaken the 'barrier' to the acceptance of low-paid and tedious work which welfare provision provides for those excluded from the labour market. To date at least, it has been considered too dangerous politically to 'force' people into low-paid work by the automatic withdrawal of benefit; but the drift is definitely in that direction, and has come closest to implementation in the recent policy changes on youth unemployment.

The Conservative Government initially used the Manpower Services Commission to oversee its policy in this area. In a series of initiatives, the long-term unemployed were subject to limited amounts of training and increasing pressure to take low-paid work, and the young unemployed were forced into temporary posts paying little more than unemployment benefit. The MSC had 34 programmes in operation in 1987, among which the biggest were the Youth Training Scheme for the 16–18-year-olds, and the Community Programme and Restart scheme for the long-term unemployed. Details of those are given in Table 5.4.

Between 1981 and 1986 employers were paid a £15-a-week subsidy per job on condition that weekly wages for young workers were held below first £55, then later £65. Half a million young

Table 5.4 Main MSC Training Programmes, 1987

Scheme	Type of training	Weekly 'wage' (£)	Numbers (000s)
Youth Training Scheme	2 years' work experience and training for 16–18-year-olds	31.75	362
Community Programme	Temporary work in the community for long-term unemployed	67.00	245
Restart	Counselling and training for those unemployed for more than six months	—	700
Job Training Scheme	Six months' work experience and training with an employer for unemployed people under 25	29.35	110

Source: Sunday Times, 31st May 1987, p.76.

workers were taken out of Wages Council cover in 1986; and in
1988 any worker voluntarily leaving work lost benefit for six
months, in a move explicitly designed to keep workers in low-paid
work, once forced there by the pressure of the new rules governing
training and benefit for the unemployed. This was not quite
'workfare' in the American sense—with its compulsory working
for benefit—but it is getting close. Under the Restart Scheme, the
pressure on the long-term unemployed to take low-paid employment is clearly evident; and the threat of benefit loss is often
enough—not simply to take people off the unemployment
register, but to keep wages low among workers whom these
'restarted' unemployed could replace. For 'neither YTS nor the
CP creates a single job for participants. They simply redistribute
the burden of unemployment through schemes of temporary
"work" and "training". In many cases the MSC schemes have
taken over real jobs and turned them into poorly paid "work
experience" instead' (Benn and Fairley 1986, p.10). In this way
Thatcher policy gets the best of both worlds for the employing
class: a diminution of the burden of maintaining the unemployed,
and a malleable low-paid underclass available for intensified
exploitation.

So the Government has steadily—drip by drip—tried to force
the poor to accept low-paid employment by altering the terms on
which unemployment benefit is made available to them; and it has,
at the same time, steadily eroded the range of benefits available by
right to the sick, disabled and old within the labour force. The
amount of resources available for personal social services has been
restricted consistently by this Conservative Government. Social
security fraud has been pursued with a vigour notable for its
absence in the equivalent pursuit of tax evasion by the rich.
Condemnations of benefit 'scrounging' and the 'dependency
culture' have been made regularly by Conservative leaders; and
qualitative shifts have been made in social policy 'designed to
reassert individualism, self-reliance and family responsibility, and
to reverse the collective social provision of the post-war era'
(Gough 1983, p.155). Government policy changes here have
derived from concerns wider than just the question of industrial
relations reform. A government capable of cutting housing benefit
to the poor in the same month (in 1988) that it abolished all rates
of income tax over 40% is visibly driven by its loyalty to the rich,

and its belief in privilege, just as strongly as it is by a belief in the capacity of labour markets to 'clear' if only the price of labour falls low enough. But its philosophy of 'the enterprise culture' links the two concerns: a belief (or at least a claim) that any wealth taking at the top will 'trickle down' in the form of initiatives by highly-motivated entrepreneurs to create new job opportunities for the less enterprising people at the bottom of the social ladder. The social security changes, in addition to easing the tax burden on the successful, also help to 'encourage' the less successful to take whatever jobs are on offer.

After all, as Reg Prentice, the Minister for Social Security, said in 1979, 'if you believe economic salvation can only be achieved by rewarding success and the national income is not increasing, then you have no alternative but to make the unsuccessful poorer' (cited in Walker and Walker 1987, p.8). If you believe in markets, you can justify that belief to yourself. 'Deregulation' sounds like a good idea for the poor if you believe that poverty results from too much state intervention. On that view, you are actively helping the poor if, as this Government has done, you reduce Wage Council cover, do away with the fair wage resolution, weaken the trade unions, and curb the factory inspectorate. But if markets do not work in this way—if the absence of state action creates inequality—then all these changes can only make matters worse for the poor: and they have. For in reality, and when all the legitimating rhetoric has been put on one side, this Government has not really been inactive and deregulating. It has been regulative in quite a different way. It has actually and actively:

> . . . pursued a dual wage strategy. On the one hand, high salaries linked to profits have been encouraged and taxes have been cut to enhance them, while, on the other hand, low wages have been stimulated—by privatisation, the abolition of Wage Councils, and by cutting some social security benefits—as a means of increasing profitability. Rather than sharing in prosperity, increased riches for some have been at the expense of the pauperisation of others.
>
> (Walker 1987, p.3)

The result, of course, has been that the poor have grown in number, and become steadily poorer relative to the rest of the community since 1979. Despite the seven years of economic growth since 1981, families in the bottom tenth of the income ladder have actually seen their real incomes *drop* in that period, by anything between 9.7% and a staggering 27.2%, depending on their number of children. The number of people on poverty level Supplementary Benefit doubled between 1979 and 1984 (from 4 million to 8 million) at the very time when only 3% of the vast reductions in the burden of income tax (cuts of £1,200 million overall between 1979 and 1986) were finding their way to the bottom 15% of income tax payers. Inequalities have widened too among those still in employment. The median rise in income (after inflation) between 1979 and 1987 was 11.2%; but for the top 10% the rise was 22.3%, for the bottom 10% only 3.7%. Thatcherism, that is, has brought greater inequality, not just between those in work and those without paid employment, but also within the ranks of the employed themselves—'so much so that the poorest workers are now markedly more worse off compared to high earners than they were 100 years ago when pay statistics were first gathered' (Piachaud 1987, p.21).

The impact of these increases in unemployment, low pay and poverty has been unevenly distributed. It has fallen unevenly between regions. 'Broadly speaking since 1979 the South has prospered and the North has been allowed to decline' (Winyard 1987, p.39); and the regional unemployment figures demonstrate that as visibly as any figures can (see Table 5.5).

Table 5.5   Regional Unemployment, January 1987

Region	% of working population registered unemployed
North	16.9
North-West	14.3
Yorkshire and Humberside	13.8
West Midlands	13.8
East Midlands	11.4
South-West	10.4
East Anglia	9.3
South-East	8.5
Northern Ireland	19.3
Scotland	15.1
Wales	14.3
UNITED KINGDOM	11.9

Source: Winyard (1987) p.41.

Pay levels, length of unemployment, the scale of poverty, and a whole range of education, health and mortality figures also settled, in the Thatcher years, into this consistent regional pattern. Within regions, too, economic inequalities intensified. 'At the beginning of 1987 there were 18 towns and cities in England . . . that had an official unemployment rate of over 20% (ibid., p.41); and these included towns in the South-West such as Newquay as well as in the North and Midlands. Outside England, in the rest of the United Kingdom, urban unemployment rates could be higher still. Five towns in Northern Ireland had unemployment rates of over 30% in 1987, with Strabane highest at 39.1%. Winchester, by comparison, was 5.2% (ibid., p.42).

These inequalities, though they manifested themselves spatially, were and are in reality social ones. The burden of rising poverty in Thatcher's Britain has fallen most heavily on particular social groups: on white working class men to a significant degree, of course, but far more on white working class women, and on both men and women in certain ethnic communities. Women in employment were, and remain, heavily concentrated in industries which pay low wages, and in low grades even within industries which do not. Full-time unemployment among women has risen slightly faster in the 1980s than among men, as women have been pushed even more into part-time work, with its low hourly rates and fewer employee rights. The statutory rights of women workers (on maternity leave in particular) have been eroded in the Conservatives' employment legislation; and the general pressure on women to cope at home (with heavier levels of male unemployment, the diminished value of social security benefits in real terms, and the rundown of public care for the old and disabled) has also intensified. In a patriarchal society such as this one, 'women bear the brunt of managing poverty on a day to day basis . . . indeed the lower the household income, the more likely it is that this responsibility will rest with women'. As Caroline Glendinning correctly observes, 'whether they live alone or with a partner, on benefits or low earnings, it is usually women who are responsible for making ends meet and for managing the debts which result when they don't' (Glendinning 1987, p.60). In this the Thatcher achievement is as paradoxical as it is cruel: that the first woman Prime Minister should have presided over a growth in poverty, the burden of which falls most heavily on the women among the poor.

Black communities too have been disproportionately hit by the creation of dual labour markets and an underclass of the poor in Thatcherite Britain. Part of this is straightforwardly structural, in that black workers even in the long post-war boom occupied low-paid, unskilled and dirty jobs in the main—jobs whose number and rates of pay have been particularly affected by Conservative policies on public sector retrenchment, the privatisation of public services and reduction of Wage Council cover. The vast majority of black people in Britain were already poor in 1979, and have been the victims of the intensification of income inequality in the years since then. But their location in that position in the class structure reflects the racism which is deep in British social structure and attitudes—a racism to which the Thatcher Government has contributed with its jingoism, its Nationality Act, and its hostility to any local attempts at positive discrimination. The result, in economic terms, has been disproportionately high levels of black unemployment, and persistently low rates of earnings by black workers who managed to hang on to their jobs.

> By the Spring of 1985 the unemployment rate for black men had more than trebled and was almost twice that for white men—20% and 11% respectively. Among black women it was 19%, compared to 10% for white women, and for black 16–24 year olds it was 33% compared with 16% for young white people.   (Arnott 1987, p.62)

Unemployment rates for particular communities were often even higher—Arnott reports a local Liverpool survey in 1986 with black unemployment rates of 80% (ibid., p.63); and black workers in employment were still heavily concentrated in low-wage sectors:

> For example, black men are almost four times as likely as white men to be working in the hotel and catering industry, a sector notorious for its low wages and poor working conditions, and one where the demise of wage council protection for young people may lead to wages being cut even further. The figures for black and white women in the hotel and catering industry are identical, reflecting the low status work which many women, whatever their colour, are subjected to.   (ibid., p.68)

The Thatcher years have left black workers in Britain trapped in poverty—jobless or low-paid—and living in the main in the inner city areas from which the rate-capping Conservatives have diverted resources. British 'Bantustans', as well as a labour force divided between a core and a periphery, are major legacies of a decade of sustained Conservative policy.

V

There can be no doubt that this division of the labour force into a privileged core and a vast disorganised periphery has helped to undermine further the industrial power of the labour movement as a whole. Certainly the trade unions have found no mechanism for linking effectively the concerns of these two groups, nor for uniting with them the vast ranks of the unemployed. The removal of corporatist institutions, the toughening of labour law against sympathy action and political strikes, and the intensification of competition in both the product and labour markets, have left different groups of workers to struggle for better conditions in isolation one from another. For many workers, either employed, on the dole, or dependent on other sections of the welfare system, the daily struggle to cope has absorbed their entire energies, so that their involvement in any public form of protest and resistance has been significantly eroded. But the Thatcher Government has not managed to break resistance in total. What it has done is to guarantee, at least for the moment, that resistance when it comes is episodic and contained.

The only 'revolt' of the dispossessed that the Thatcher years have so far witnessed has been the revolt in the cities in 1980 and 1981. There was a moment—in the hot summer of 1981—when it looked as though Conservative pressure on the urban poor had been more intense than either they could tolerate or the State's repressive arm could handle. A taste of what was to come occurred in the St Paul's riot in Bristol in April 1980; and this was followed by riots in Brixton in April 1981 and by riots in Southall, Liverpool, Manchester, and a whole string of other Northern and Midland cities and towns in July 1981. The focus of rioting was invariably the local police; but beneath the immediate trigger lay—and still remain—layers of frustration and poverty among black and white youth trapped in ghettoised unemployment and social deprivation. Thatcher's inner cities have been quiet since, but the underlying causes of those riots remain, as a slumbering reminder of the precariousness of the social stability over which the Thatcher Government so confidently presides.

Workers in the core of the labour market—better protected, better paid, more self-confident, and with more to lose—have been more regularly resistant. One of the Thatcher Government's regular claims is its impact on the level of industrial disputes among just such workers. In fact, there has been a lot of industrial militancy since 1979, most of it by public sector workers, against the application of Thatcherite policies to particular industries and public services. The 'defeat' of public sector unionism was achieved only through a series of major national stoppages which inflated the strike figures: of steelworkers in 1980, civil servants in 1981, health workers in 1982, of miners in 1984–5, and of teachers in 1985–6–7. The place of 1981–85 in the overall history of strikes in the United Kingdom is given in Table 5.6.

Table 5.6 Stoppages of Work Due to Industrial Disputes in the UK

	No. of stoppages	No. of workers involved	Working days lost
1966–70	2,691	1,398,000	5,531,000
1971–75	2,559	1,369,000	13,045,000
1976–80	2,120	1,663,000	12,854,000
1981–85	1,255	1,268,000	9,188,000

Source: Jackson (1987) p.70.

But when these public sector strikes are excluded from the strike statistics, it is clear that the incidence of strike action elsewhere has fallen away. The number of recorded disputes in 1985—900— was the lowest for any year since 1938; and though the number of days lost in 1984 was the highest since the General Strike, 82% of that figure came from the miners' strike. 'Public sector disputes have accounted for over half the working days lost in major disputes in the 1980s, a percentage not equalled since the early 1970s' (Longstreth 1988, p.15) and one that reflected both the drop in private sector strike activity and the Government's own intransigence as an employer. In the very period in which wave upon wave of public sector employees were confronting their government as employer, 'there was a substantial decline in manual strike action among establishments in the private manufacturing sector'; a decline that was most marked, between 1980 and 1984, in vehicle construction, metal goods and metal engineering, rubber and plastics (Millward and Stevens 1985, pp. 265–6). Teachers, nurses and other white-collar workers showed an enhanced propensity to strike during the early Thatcher years, while more seasoned campaigners among manual workers in the private sector did not.

Thatcherism has not brought industrial peace so much as altered the distribution and intensity of strike action between sectors, and thereby between classes of workers. There is clear evidence now that, in the private sector as well as in the public, industrial militancy is quickening again. Thatcherite attacks on the National Health Service still face serious resistance from the nursing unions; and their campaign in 1988, not simply for wages but for extra resources for the NHS, clearly had the support of very wide swathes of public opinion. Less generally popular, but equally militant in 1988, have been car workers and seamen. The strikes against P & O by the National Union of Seamen may well be the latest in a long line of doomed attempts to resist large-scale redundancies and industrial rundown; but those in the car industry cannot be seen in that light. At Rover, at Vauxhall and at Fords in the winter of 1987–88, car workers reminded the Government again of the residual industrial strength of heavily unionised manual workers, and underscored the reality which Thatcherism has not yet changed: namely that as the recession eases, a drop in militancy previously policed by large-scale unemployment will begin inexorably to fade. What the supporters of the Thatcher experiment have often taken as a permanent diminution in working class militancy may yet prove to have been a temporary and contingent one. By failing to break the industrial organisation of British workers, by refusing to finance the training of sufficient skilled people, and by tolerating (and indeed encouraging) the development of a dual labour market, Thatcherism may yet fall victim to the militancy of core workers whose bargaining position has been strengthened by such parsimony. For the Thatcher Government has helped to create a core of workers able and willing to keep its earnings rising faster than inflation. In 1988 earnings are still outstripping inflation by as much as 4%—evidence indeed of the extent to which the Conservative Government has so far failed in its strategic objective of diminishing permanently the industrial power of the organised working class.

As yet, with the exception of the NUM, much of that organised working class has not been led with any foresight or courage. What Thatcherism has not produced is a militant trade union leadership; and here the legal changes of the Thatcher years, and the unemployment, have combined to keep national trade union leadership firmly in line. Mass unemployment, new labour laws, and general state hostility may have provoked determined resistance from individual unions—the NUM is again the prime example—but more generally they have stimulated an acceptance of the 'new realism' both by individual union leadership (of the engineers and electricians in particular) and by the TUC leadership as a whole. There was a brief moment of radical rhetoric from the latter—an initial Wembley strategy in 1982 forbidding acceptance by affiliated unions of government funds for ballotting, and promising assistance to unions sued under the new law. But these shades of 1971 and 1972 did not survive the Conservatives' election victory in 1983. Nor did they surface in other than rhetorical support by the TUC either for the National Graphical Association at Warrington in 1983, the NUM in its long dispute, or in 1986 when the print unions were faced with Murdoch's provocative move of his print works to Wapping.

Instead, and inexorably, the 'new realism' involved a more (in the case of Eric Hammond) or less (in the case of Norman Willis) enthusiastic acceptance of single-union deals, pendulum arbitration, and operation within the new and highly constricting limits of the Tory legal code. Unions in breach of court rulings (and suffering sequestration of their funds) received no substantial aid from fellow trade union leaders, but were allowed to go down to defeat alone. Beyond waiting for a Labour Government to replace the dreaded legislation, the national trade union leadership in the 1980s came up with no practical solution to the Conservative legal onslaught, and certainly eschewed any notion of a generalised struggle of the early 1970s type against the quite crippling legal barriers to sympathy action by fellow trade unionists. Instead, national trade union officials began to lower their demands (accepting in the main the permanence of statutory ballots, so surrendering the ideological initiative to Thatcher) whilst reactivating their social contract with a new Labour Party leadership which was equally in retreat before the Conservative onslaught. Both wings of the labour movement seem to have conceded by 1983 'that the "politicisation" and "juridification" of industrial relations are no longer reversible, and that policy must therefore focus on changes in the content and direction of the law rather than on vain attempts at its exclusion' (Hyman 1987, p.108). The Labour Party went to its third election defeat in a row armed with a social contract between itself and the national trade union leadership which mixed proposals on new workers' and union rights (to information, consultation and representation) with proposals to extend secret ballotting before strikes and when electing union officials. This represented a considerable shift towards Thatcherite specifications of what constitutes proper union government, and as Richard Hyman observed, constituted a remarkably rapid and substantial revision of 'the conception of the role of the state and the law in industrial relations' (ibid., p.104) by both wings of the movement.

But it would not do to end this chapter on such a bleak note for the Left, not least because there has recently been one limited but refreshing reminder of the residual strength of British trade unionism—one indicator of the defensive tenacity still alive there, on which the eventual reconstruction of a radical labour movement will be able to build. That is to be found in the union reaction to Part III of the 1984 Trade Union Act, requiring unions with a political fund to ballot their members on its retention. The Government proposed this reform, as it did others in the 1984 Act, as part of its campaign to 'give the unions back to their members'. We have already commented on the adequacy in general of that claim; and here we should merely note that the Labour Party was understandably fairly certain that what the proposals represented instead was 'a transparent attempt to cause financial difficulties to the Labour Party and to undermine the Opposition's effectiveness' (John Smith, cited in Steele et al. 1986, p.448). In fact the definition of 'political expenditure' adopted in the Bill was sufficiently wide as possibly to jeopardise the capacity of unions to launch any effective general political campaign against government legislation; and when this was recognised by union members, support for the retention of political funds grew.

No doubt the Government would have seen a pattern of voting more empathetic to its partisan purposes if it had managed to persuade the rank and file of the unions affected that the term 'political' referred in this context only to the funding of political parties. But it did not. For the TUC set up its own co-ordinating committee, which focused its defence of political funds, not on the Labour Party issue, but behind the more general slogan 'Yes to a voice in Parliament'. Not surprisingly, Government ministers were quick to accuse the unions of using misleading arguments, and of slipping in support for the Labour Party under the cover of a false fear about general political campaigning. But for once in a clash of voices, it was the Government's which failed to get through. 'Between May 1985 and 31 March 1986, 37 unions affiliated to the TUC with political funds held successful ballots for their retention, as did one union not in membership of the TUC' (Steele *et al.* 1986, p.456); and two unions without political funds actually voted to create them! Altogether 3.6 million trade unionists voted, in elections that involved participation rates of between 50% and 70%; and of that 3.6 million, an amazingly high 83% cast their vote in favour of retention.

Of course, it would be unwise to draw from this pattern of voting

> conclusions about unionists' support for the Labour Party. Many members who did not vote Labour in 1979 and 1983 voted in support of the political fund, and there is no evidence from recent polls and election results to suggest that all, or even a significant proportion, have switched their allegiance to Labour. Virtually all trade unionists interviewed were agreed that it had been strategically correct not to stress the role of the Labour Party in the campaign and to concentrate instead on the political implications of matters that arise in the workplace and that have a direct implication for the workforce.   (Blackwell and Terry 1987, p.642)

Nonetheless,this result constituted a rare and, for the Left, encouraging demonstration of the limited impact of Thatcherite initiatives. It made clear, as few other things have been able to do since 1979, that the Conservative onslaught on unionism can be blocked, that anti-Thatcherite forces can win. It therefore constitutes a suitable backcloth against which to consider, finally, to what degree, and by what methods, those anti-Thatcherite forces can regroup and conquer political power in Britain in the 1990s. The politics of industrial relations in Britain in the 1960s and 1970s were dominated by Labour. In the 1980s dominance has lain with the Conservatives. It is time now to take stock, and look forward, to anticipate the likely politics of industrial relations in the years to come.

6

Taking Stock and Moving On

Prognosis is a dangerous exercise in areas as fluid as national politics, but some pointers need to be made, and some tasks suggested, if the future is not merely to be anticipated, but also to be shaped. What we have established thus far gives us some of these pointers; and from them it should be possible, in a tentative way at least, to indicate the range of options available for political forces in this area in the decade to come. Two political phenomena in particular stand out as likely to be dominant in the first half of the 1990s: the strength and self-confidence of Conservatism, and the persistent crisis of Labour. So let us examine the likely impact of each of these, before seeing whether—from their interplay— new options of a more attractive kind might emerge.

I

The future of industrial relations and its politics will definitely be shaped—and indeed initially will primarily be shaped—by Thatcherite control of the State, and by the penetration of Thatcherite ideas into the minds of wide sections of the British working class. Working class Conservatism, both the party kind and more generalised political moderation, will continue to be a major problem for left-wing forces in Britain as the century closes. So it is important to understand the long-term roots and more immediate causes of that conservatism. There is, of course, nothing new about British workers voting for the Conservative Party. From 1867 Disraeli was able to see a Conservative constituency in the working class which he was willing cautiously and incrementally to enfranchise—'angels in marble' as he put it—Conservative working class voters who were, in the event, heavily concentrated among non-unionised employees in small-firm and rural industries. Frank Parkin explained their vote a long time ago as the product of the penetration into the working class of dominant values and symbols, a penetration having its greatest impact where 'barriers' to it were at their weakest. He even produced a diagram (see Figure 6.1) to capture the notion of these barriers against Conservative voting, drawing them as circles around the voter's electoral cross (Parkin 1966, p.285). The 'circles' he emphasised were those of working class communities and large-scale factories. Today one might add trade union membership and public sector employment as other barriers, but certainly part of the Conservative working class vote is, in Parkin's sense, an old, well-established, unprotected vote which Labour has never managed to shift.

However, the recent electoral and ideological impact of Thatcherite Conservatism has been about more than that. The Conservative Party under Margaret Thatcher has not only *inherited* a Tory working class vote. It has also *created* one, by picking up support from traditional Labour supporters; and has in addition had a more diffuse ideological impact beyond its now widened

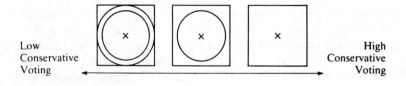

Figure 6.1

electoral base, shaping the agenda, and providing the categories within which even Labour voters have come to approach their politics. Those categories, as we have seen, are profoundly Liberal ones—in an almost Gladstonian sense of that term. It is this Liberal revival, as well as Conservative electoral success, with which the Left in the 1990s will have to deal, and which we therefore, in the 1980s, need to be able to explain.

The explanation lies, I think, in two places. It lies partly in the long-established moderation of working class politics in Britain, to which we will come later in this chapter. But it lies, too, and more immediately, as we saw in the last chapter, in the character of Thatcherism as *hegemonic politics*.

The Italian Marxist Antonio Gramsci used the notion of hegemony to explain the stability of the capitalist social order, to clarify the nature of political leadership within that order, and to specify the nature of left-wing politics which such capitalist hegemony makes essential; and his arguments still hold the key to much of what is happening around us now, half a century after his death. In essence, his argument was the old one that the State does not rule by force alone, but must win genuine popular support for its politics and its social order, and win that support not simply from those privileged by that order, but from those exploited by it too. Put in the language of Gramscian Marxism, a hegemonic state is one which consolidates around itself a bloc of classes, and articulates to them and for them a unifying and legitimising set of ideas which become the common sense of the entire society. Each age in which one party (and its associated bloc of classes) is hegemonic is thus dominated by one common sense; and hegemony declines as that 'common sense' loses its purchase on the minds of its people. That hegemony is a class hegemony when (and to the degree that) within the bloc of classes consolidated in alliance by the State, one class rules: by being able to project its class interests as the 'neutral' interests of the society as a whole, by being able to absorb and partly accommodate (through genuine concessions) the conflicting interests of subordinate classes, and by being able to mobilise institutions in the state and civil society to articulate and reproduce the consensual patterns that its dominance requires. Such a ruling class, precisely because it is able 'through ideological struggle to articulate to its hegemonic principle the majority of the important ideological elements in a given society', creates stability

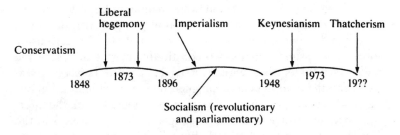

Figure 6.2

through its capacity to 'create a determinant conception of the
world and to establish a certain definition of reality which is
accepted by those over whom hegemony is exercised' (Mouffe
1980, p.173).

This understanding of the nature of hegemonic power within
capitalism gives us a particular way of reading recent British
history and of situating Thatcherism within it. It suggests that we
should look for the dominant hegemonic package in each epoch of
capitalist development, and for the bloc of classes united around
it. That might give us, in the British case, a picture such as shown
in Figure 6.2.

In each long wave of capitalist expansion, ideas and classes
struggled for dominance. In the first phase of British industrial
capitalism—its brief period of world monopoly—liberal ideas (of
individualism, the neutrality of markets, the nightwatchman state,
and the possibility of obtaining 'a fair day's wage for a fair day's
work') replaced earlier conservative ideas in dominance. These
Liberal ideas were carried into history as the world view of a rising
industrial bourgeoisie which had no need of state assistance, and
which was economically sufficiently strong to 'incorporate' at least
the skilled sections of the working class into its vision (through its
fusion of the Victorian labour aristocracy into a permanent if
subordinate position within the Lib–Lab coalition of Gladstonian
Liberalism). After 1873, and particularly in the 1890s, as international competition quickened and social unrest grew, that
hegemonic bloc slowly disintegrated. Disintegration is the key
word here, for 'bits' of Liberal thought remained in the common
sense of the age (the ideas of individualism and market neutrality
in particular) just as 'bits' of the earlier Conservatism (of the
nation and the family) remained from the pre-Victorian period.

But this package as a whole did not remain in place, and certainly not in dominance. After a long period of political struggle, social unrest and economic decline, the Liberal Party—its organising force—split asunder as its two constitutive classes diverged: the industrial bourgeoisie eventually moved to a more statist conservatism, and the working class realigned politically behind a Labour Party which was profoundly liberal in its origins. It took the interwar years to resolve both those realignments—of business to the Conservatives, and workers to Labour. The Labour Party–working class realignment in particular was not completed until 1945, by a party whose first generation of leaders all began as Liberals, and which by 1945 had had to struggle successfully not only against the Liberal Party on its Right, but also against more revolutionary specifications of working class goals coming from the Marxist groups to its Left.

Between the wars no ideology dominated, and no bloc of classes was truly hegemonic. On the contrary, class struggle was intense, unpredictable and violent as on the world stage Fascist and Communist visions and movements clashed, and the liberal coalition slowly regrouped around the notion of a managed capitalism (in the New Deal in the USA, in Macmillan's *Third Way*, and in Keynes's *General Theory of Employment*). In Britain, liberal ideas persisted, the imperial solution to the decline of industry after 1870 remained intact, and the Left was split on the question of what kinds of coalition, if any, were appropriate for the interests of British workers. But by 1945 most of these disputes had been resolved, or were on the way to being resolved. In Britain the Labour Party had emerged as the dominant vehicle of a new hegemonic package—one organised around Keynesianism— and resting on the fusion of the two same basic classes —industrial capital and organised labour—which had earlier underpinned Victorian Liberalism, but which were now united in a post-war settlement of full employment, welfarism and the persistence of private capital. That new package emerged out of Liberalism. Keynes himself was a Liberal, as we saw; and Labourism as a whole made no sharp break with the dominant ideas of either the Gladstonian or the Imperial past: the ideas of market and nation, individual and property, family and labour.

So, as we saw in detail in the previous chapter, Thatcherism must be understood as yet another hegemonic package; and the ease of its penetration must be seen as deriving from the persistence of basic liberal values and ideas in the society it inherited. For the ideological onslaught launched by the Conservative Party since 1975—'The Great Moving Right Show' as Stuart Hall has called it (Hall 1983)—was exactly in the Gramscian mould, as we noted above. It was an attempt to articulate to its hegemonic principle (of unbridled individualism) all the important ideological elements in the society, and to establish a certain definition of reality as the common sense of an entire age. The establishment of that particular definition was, and is, a possibility because in the past (and as we saw in Chapter 4) the Labour Party has never inserted into that 'common sense' a qualitatively different conception of the world to that laid out first by Conservatism and then by Liberalism. Thatcherite definitions stand fair to succeed to the degree that, and until, the Left is capable of generating and propagating such a qualitative break. Thatcherism as hegemonic politics, that is, requires of the Left nothing less than the politics of counter-hegemony.

That such politics are possible derives from the other feature of hegemonic politics visible in the picture: the fact that hegemonic principles *lose* their dominance as the contradictory interests of the classes supporting them emerge to undermine their credibility in the minds of significant groupings in the population as a whole. Conservative ideas of 'the nation' and 'the family' still have their power because they map directly onto a world organised internationally as a set of competing nation states and internally as privatised domestic units of reproduction and consumption. But Liberal ideas of free trade and limited state action did not in the end survive the loss of world monopoly dominance by British industry on which they were initially generalised; and, as we saw, Keynesian corporatism did not survive the economic crisis of the 1970s. The hold of each was 'weakened' by the emergence of problems: of international competition and working class unrest (in the case of nineteenth-century Liberalism) and of industrial decline and generalised stagflation (for Keynesian corporatism). These were problems with which Liberal or Keynesian ideas could not easily cope, and over which their supporting bloc of classes began increasingly to diverge. But changing conditions only weakened their hold; and, once weakened, they had to be brought down by political initiatives by their opponents (by the 'tariff campaign' of inter-war Conservatism and the rising tide of Labour—in the case of Liberalism—and by Thatcherite monetarism in the more recent case). What we have to do now, therefore, is to *locate* the conditions which could weaken Thatcherism, and *explore* the political initiatives which could sweep it away. Such a set of exercises—of location and exploration— is a particularly appropriate thing to do here because ultimately neither will be possible without a full understanding of the politics of industrial relations in Britain in the 1990s.

II

Counter-hegemonic initiatives require ideas and political leadership, both of which we will discuss shortly. But they also require social forces available for mobilisation, chinks in the support for the dominant order into which new ideas can be inserted. A counter-hegemonic strategy is still a possibility in late twentieth-century Britain because those chinks exist in abundance. This is most immediately obvious in electoral terms. Thatcherite support at the polls is still a minority support. In 1979, the Conservative share of the vote was 43.9%; in 1983 it was 42.4%; and in 1987 still only 42.3%. Thatcherism has so far 'neither produced a new national–popular consensus nor created a new organic power bloc' (Jessop *et al.* 1984, p.41). The attempt to do so is still on, of course, but as yet its success is, at most, only a partial one.

Moreover, though Thatcherite Conservatism presents itself as a sharp rupture with the post-war social democratic consensus, it is clear that not all the institutional initiatives of the social democratic period have lost popular support. It is true that, as we saw in Chapter 4, publicly owned industries clearly generate no mass loyalty, and have not since at least the mid-1950s. 'Private' ownership of industry and finance (which of course actually means real control of industry and finance by a privileged few) remains legitimate in popular eyes in ways that 'state ownership' does not. The Labour Party lost that argument in the 1950s, and no longer really believes it itself; and has not yet found a way of guaranteeing that publicly owned firms and industries can be efficient (and sensitive to consumer interests) in ways that small private firms have to be and big private monopolies pretend to be. But 'private ownership' and 'profit making' still have no generalised legitimacy in the area of welfare provision. People accept it as 'fair' to make a profit out of selling wage goods, but not out of providing health care, education, and basic pensions. Nor, as the Thatcherites found in 1988, are people in general comfortable with reductions in social security benefits to the poor at the moment when tax relief is being extended to the very rich. There is still an underlying sense of morality, fair play and egalitarianism in British popular culture which social democracy in its heyday reinforced, and which Thatcherite individualism has not yet found a way of eroding.

It is in these areas of welfare provision that the Thatcherite attack on social democracy has had to proceed with the greatest stealth, incrementally undermining the viability (and hence generalised legitimacy) of the National Health Service by a mixture of limited public funding and the encouragement of parallel private health care behind a rhetoric of extending 'choice'. Yet people are not stupid. They know that choice in private health care depends on income. Even after a decade of Thatcherism, popular support for NHS hospitals, nurses and doctors remains. Too many people cannot afford health care to allow any full-frontal assault on state welfare provision; and because this is so, it is one obvious area of popular attitudes in which a revival of left-wing fortunes can begin. For the NHS is more than an area from which the market has to be excluded: it is also a model of how community-focused, rather than market-inspired, provision can be organised. It is these prefigurative socialist qualities which make it so dangerous to Thatcherism—and yet so difficult for the Thatcher Government entirely to dismantle.

The legacy of social democracy in Britain is not just a set of attitudes and institutions. The social democratic dominance of post-war Britain also involved a major restructuring of the distribution of occupations; and brought into existence related, though distinguishable, groups of workers who remain remarkably unenthusiastic about a right-wing political project built on privatisation and the market. Social democracy created a massive public sector, largely (though not exclusively) geared to welfare provision.

Workers at all levels in that sector show a more marked propensity than do workers elsewhere to vote Labour and to remain resistant to policies whose logic is rooted in the competitive relationships of the private market. All the indicators suggest that Conservative support is lowest, within all strata, among those who work for government agencies of any sort, and especially among workers farthest away from the private accumulation process: in the welfare bureaucracies which look after those whom the private sector discards as unwanted. All the indicators suggest, too, an increase in anti-Conservative voting the further *down* the state bureaucracies we go. Public sector managers may still be structurally predisposed to be conservative in their politics. Public sector professionals, white-collar workers and manual grades are not. Union membership is particularly high among these workers. So, too, is voting Labour and a willingness to strike against Conservative policy and mobilise on issues beyond the workplace (from health cuts to nuclear weapons).

In particular, professional and white-collar workers in the public sector have grown in number and self-confidence since 1945; they now constitute Labour's most solid basis of support. As we saw in Chapter 4, a middle class Left of predominantly state employees exists in Britain as one of social democracy's most abiding legacies. It is a middle class Left which is predisposed by its position in the social and economic structure of contemporary capitalism to challenge Thatcherite hegemony, to do the intellectual homework necessary to replace it, and to provide the activists for the Labour Party, and for many of the single-issue campaigns which Thatcherism has been unable to remove. 'Indeed, if Labour voting is taken as an index of radicalism, the middle class Left—constituting as it does some 30% of all middle class votes—is in percentage terms as significant a political fact in contemporary Britain as is working class support for the Conservatives' (Coates 1984b, p.132). The same point can be put in more qualitative, less quantitative, terms. Social democracy has created a large bloc of people earning their living away from any direct and regular contact with the production and sale of commodities by private firms; and as Thatcherism has attempted to generalise the imperatives of that form of production across the society as a whole, resistance has been greatest where commodification has been least.

Of course, the electoral success of the Conservative Party under

Margaret Thatcher has been built elsewhere—on an extension of Conservative voting outside the public sector, particularly among the skilled sections of the working class employed by private industry: but that strategy, too, has its underside. The economic policies of the Conservative Government since 1979—moving with the grain of private capital's dominant patterns of industrial relations, as we have seen—has involved a restructuring of the entire working class. It has reinforced the industrial position of well-organised white male skilled workers, but at the price of undermining the industrial position and earning power of large numbers of other workers. There is a new and extensive underclass of the poor in Thatcher's Britain. Many of those poor people lie outside the labour market altogether: poor because of the restricted levels of social provision and the extended scale of unemployment in Britain since 1979—poor because of government determination to force them into low-paid work by holding benefits lower still. But many of the poor are actually inside the employed labour force—in the rapidly growing 'peripheral' jobs (low-paid, low-skilled, and largely non-unionised) that cushion the position of skilled workers. Female labour of all ages and colours, the white male young, and black labour both male and female, young and old, are disproportionately represented there; and among these groups Conservative voting remains a minority sport.

Nor is it yet clear whether Conservative support among skilled workers is necessarily a permanent feature of electoral life in Britain in the 1990s. There is one specific and one general reason why it may not be so. The specific reason is the fragility of the economic recovery now under way in Thatcherite Britain. Thatcherism faces a real contradiction here: to the degree that its economic strategy does generate economic growth and competitive strength, it enhances the confidence of the well-organised work groups that its industrial strategy was designed to undermine. There is plenty of evidence—in the rate of industrial earnings and the revival of industrial militancy—to suggest that Thatcherism has not yet broken the power of organised labour at the point of production. If it has not, the industrial recovery on which its long-term electoral future depends is still in jeopardy.

That recovery is precarious in any case, depending as it does on the cushioning of an enormous balance of payments deficit by oil revenues and the earnings of the City. The first of these will go.

The second will doubtless follow; and then industrial workers, no less than already anti-Thatcherite public sector employees, will experience in full the *failure* of Thatcher's long-term attempt to revitalise British industrial capital. Economic success, while it lasts, bolsters the self-confidence of skilled and organised sections of the working class, and keeps alive the tradition and experience of industrial militancy, if not of political radicalism. Economic failure, when it comes, must weaken the Conservative hold on skilled working class votes. Thatcherite individualism—with its emphasis on living off the market and looking after private interests by determined action—is ironically helping to keep alive, among workers in industries doing well in the marketplace, traditions of wage militancy and shopfloor organisation; and that organisation and militancy will be loyal to Thatcher only for so long as they and she do not clash; only for so long, that is, as Britain's modest economic recovery can be made to continue.

Politics, of course, live on specifics. Conservative voting among skilled workers will not evaporate overnight. But unlike so much of what the Thatcher Conservatives have done, their hold on skilled workers' votes does run *against*, and not *with*, the tide of social processes in contemporary Britain. For there are general things going on behind the specifics, older and more endemic reasons why Thatcherite success here may well be ephemeral. The economy over which the Thatcher Government presides is still a capitalist one, and all workers within it (at whatever level of skill) must necessarily experience it as potentially radicalising. For at the heart of the capitalist labour process, for skilled workers no less than for unskilled, and for core workers no less than for peripheral ones, lies the creation and recreation of the surplus value of labour power. A capitalist economy only survives and prospers by, and to the extent that, the purchasers of labour power are able to extract from the labour they purchase a greater value than they are obliged to return to it in the form of wages; and this requirement puts in place in each and every labour process (beneath and colouring everything else that is going on there) a necessary tension between capital and labour. The owners of capital, and those who manage labour on its behalf, find themselves under a systemically-induced pressure to intensify the rate at which they extract surplus from the labour they employ, either by extending that part of the working day which is surplus to labour's own requirements, or by increasing the productivity of labour in each and every period of work. For the workers subject to managements with such concerns, this systematically-induced pressure to accumulate capital from their surplus labour manifests itself as a perennial managerial pressure to established trade-offs between effort and wages, and as a process of managerial supervision which is geared not to the workers' needs as workers but to the company's needs to produce cheaply, to produce quickly, and to produce with the minimum of waste. For when workers sell labour to a capitalist concern, they do more than surrender brain and muscle power. They also surrender their freedom of action as producing agents, and submit themselves, however reluctantly, to a managerial decision-making structure and authority system which is geared to the accumulation of profit through their labour.

Of course, in any social order, and not just in a capitalist one, co-operative effort to produce goods and services will inevitably require rules, co-ordination and the voluntary surrender (of an individual's unfettered freedom to act) to some collective specification of tasks, rewards and responsibilities. A system of industrial relations will therefore be needed in the most egalitarian and democratic system of work organisation, to resolve just these questions of collective control and individual responsibility. In essence, what capitalism adds to this necessarily co-operative nature of most work processes, and therefore to the agenda and climate of industrial relations, is a tension between the extractors and the providers of surplus value. It superimposes upon rule-making processes geared to the achievement of optimum collective effort, rules and work practices geared to intensifying the extraction of a surplus from that effort, turning work as it does so into a process experienced by those subject to it as to some degree beyond their control, and alienated from their interests. The result is that workers in a capitalist system find, and find progressively the less they occupy positions of ownership and command within the capitalist enterprise, that overwhelmingly what they have to do is *defend* themselves through negotiations around the job, a defence which has to take the form of blocking, deflecting or reversing perennial managerial attempts to shift the terms of the wage-effort bargain against them.

This pressure of capital on labour always creates a 'space' for the insertion of socialist politics, however hard anti-socialist forces try to block that space with counter-ideologies and alternative definitions of reality and interests. A Thatcherite strategy of making a virtue of this necessity—of preaching the benefit to all of competition and efficiency—works only so long as economic growth can be maintained, and only so long as the intensification of work routines can be over-compensated by the easing of limits on workers as consumers (for evidence of this 'war between citizenship and social class', see Marshall *et al.* 1985, p.279). But future trends in industrial relations in Britain suggest that this balancing act will be harder to achieve in the 1990s than it was in the 1980s. The intensification of international competition, the opening up of the European market in 1992, and the growing importance of foreign multinationals as employers in the United Kingdom, all are or will increasingly bring even skilled workers up against the instability and intensified exploitation of the late twentieth-century capitalist world market. Under international market pressures of a growing force, across British industry as a whole managerial controls on working practices are tightening, single-union deals and no-strike agreements are beginning to spread, technological innovation is quickening, and the inter-national mobility of capital is becoming more marked. No doubt the position of skilled workers will continue to be cushioned to a degree by the super-exploitation of less organised and less secure peripheral workers; but as the Thatcher Government continues to open domestic markets to the full force of foreign competition, the very strength of well-organised work groups may yet leave them vulnerable to an intensified 'employers' offensive' against their residual industrial power in Britain in the 1990s.

The potential for left-wing revival in Britain lies in the coming together of all these possible sources of dissatisfaction with Thatcherism. What is at stake is the primacy of self-definition into which people settle in the 1990s. Will they see themselves as consumers, as the Thatcher Government encourages them to do, feeling free to spend in a privatised Britain? Or will they see themselves as members of a working class forced to labour with greater intensity and less security of employment in order to make that consumption possible? Will they hold on to the importance of welfare spending and publicly-provided health and education services, or will they tolerate the privatisation of these last bastions of the old social democratic consensus? On the surface, things look easier for the Right than for the Left in the struggle to resolve those questions, and not just because the Right holds the reins of power. As we have seen, capitalism and Thatcherite Liberalism do have a strong empathy with each other, because of the way in which capital is accumulated only through exchange. Capitalism requires not just a sphere of production (in which social relationships take an unequal, class, form). It also requires a 'noisy sphere' of exchange, in which individuals are free to consume, subject only to the availability of goods and their capacity to pay. As we saw in more detail in the previous chapter, Thatcherism urges people to define themselves as consumers, not producers: consumers of anything from wage goods through tax cuts, shares, and houses, to anti-communism, law and order, and a new morality. Those definitions will predominate in the long term only (a) if that consumption is possible for its targeted groups, and (b) if the social relationships of production do not prove so traumatic as to render the image of equality of consumption visibly meaningless. And since Thatcherite consumerism is offered as the antidote to the shortcomings of social democracy, Thatcherism as a hegemonic project will work too only to the degree that (c) the legacies of social democracy do not persist against it.

Yet they do: the legacies of social democracy remain, as we have seen, in the form of popular attitudes to welfare and in the social reality of state employees. The social relations of production remain tenaciously capitalist in form: offering to left-wing causes an old working class still industrially unbroken and a new and extensive working class poor in need of non-market solutions to their poverty. The consumerism of Thatcherite Britain rests still on a shaky industrial recovery, and on the insertion of the British economy into an international economic order in which capital knows no national boundaries or loyalty, and in which the industrial strength of workers in one national economy can so easily inspire a redistribution of capital towards more supine workers elsewhere. The poverty of the unorganised working class, the industrial militancy of well-placed workers, the persistence of generalised attitudes of a social democratic kind, and the political radicalism of a new state-employed middle class, are all there for the Left to mobilise into its bloc of anti-Thatcherite forces. The social conditions for a left-wing revival exist in embryo. The question that remains is whether the political forces exist to bring that potential coalition into full life.

III

If we leave the argument at this point, only one of the two vital pieces of the jigsaw of the politics of industrial relations in the 1990s will be in place. It is clear from that 'piece' that Thatcherism, as a hegemonic project, has had a real but limited impact, and that space exists for the reconstruction of a left-wing alternative. The forces of the Right are in the ascendancy, but the foundations of their dominance are more fragile than they at first appear. Left-wing forces have the opportunity. But are they in any shape to take advantage of it, and to repel the attempt of the Social and Liberal Democrats to occupy the high ground of opposition to Thatcherite Conservatism? It is when that question is posed that a second set of issues for the 1990s begins to come into view, a set which suggests that Thatcherism is not the only barrier to a left-wing revival. Barriers exist, too, in the long-established political moderation of British workers, and in the crisis of policy and self-confidence which has overwhelmed the moderate socialist party to which most workers have given their political allegiance since 1945.

The roots of political moderation among industrial workers in Britain lie far back. Pockets of working class Conservatism were there from the 1860s, and the bulk of organised labour in late Victorian Britain gave its political loyalty to the Liberal Party, and not to the emerging forces of revolutionary socialism—represented then by the Social Democratic Federation and later by the Communist Party. Pockets of working class Toryism were balanced, between the wars, by pockets of working class communist support—especially on the coalfields of Wales and Scotland; but the Communist Party was never able to establish itself as the dominant legatee of Liberalism, as that party disintegrated after 1914. Instead, as we know, the legatee of 'Lib–Labism' proved in the British case to be the Labour Party, which established its electoral domination over the whole of organised labour by 1945; and its impact on patterns of working class consciousness both before and since, as we saw in Chapter 4, has been profoundly conservative with a small 'c', if not with a large one. Moreover, as we also saw, the linkage established between the Labour Party and its working class base in 1945 was a relatively tenuous one—based as it was on 'the special conditions of war, war mobilisation and reconstruction' (Cronin 1984, p.208)—and, as such, vulnerable to erosion almost from the moment it was created. In that erosion, changes in the industrial and social experience of workers in the post-war years played an important part, as did the failed policies of successive Labour governments after 1974. That, too, we established in Chapters 2 to 4. What we need to remember now is that the erosion of that party–class linkage did not produce any significant left-wing shift in working class political sympathies. On the contrary, the crisis of Labour moved the working class away to the Right; so the task of socialists now is that much harder. Any socialist revival in the 1990s needs not simply to wean workers away from loyalty to Labourism. It actually needs to pull them back from a centre of gravity away to Labourism's Right.

Given the magnitude of that task, it is not surprising that by the late 1970s many commentators had begun to despair of the viability of any left-wing project in Britain. And not just commentators: many politicians abandoned ship, sailing away to what they saw as easier waters in their own Social Democratic Party. And if that hit the rocks by 1988, an equivalent 'new realism' among right-wing trade union leaders did not. For material affluence, the power of capitalist culture and its mass dissemination, long-standing differences between sections of the working class, and the visible unpopularity of public ownership, all combined to persuade many left-wing commentators that *the forward march of labour* had at least temporarily halted and that, unless accommodation was made for certain of these trends, it would be halted for all time.

As we saw in Chapter 4, the notion of 'a forward march . . . halted' was Eric Hobsbawm's; and his writings—in response to a looming election defeat in 1979, and then to a series of actual defeats in the 1980s—have been an important point of reference in the debate on left-wing political strategies for the 1990s. The

original Hobsbawm essay, in 1978, emphasised structural changes
in the composition and work experience of Labour's electorate as
vital blocking factors to the spread of support for socialism. The
rise of white-collar work and state employment, generalised
affluence and the decline of the common style of proletarian life,
the presence of more women workers and ethnic minorities in the
labour force, and the persistence of sectionalism in the trade union
movement, all meant that political strategies built—as nineteenth-
century ones had been—on the assumption of the inevitable
proletarianisation of the majority of the electorate, and its
automatic solidarity with socialist politics, had to be rethought.
The Hobsbawm critique of 1978 was only embryonic, and focused
on failures of Labour Party leadership, talking of a crisis caused
for the labour movement by the failure of the Wilson governments
to win these new strands within the working class to a socialist
project. By 1983 the clarity of the Hobsbawm critique had grown,
and with clarity had come a shift of focus: away from the failures of
the Wilson years and onto developments within the Labour Party
since 1979. The spotlight by 1983 fell on the radicalism of the
Labour Left, and on divisions within the Labour Party produced
by that radicalism—on radicalism and divisions which together left
Labour's supporters alienated from Labour and vulnerable to
Thatcherism.

As defeat followed defeat in the general elections of the
Thatcher years, powerful voices inside the Labour coalition began
to argue that a moderation of policy was vital, and a coming to
terms with the conservatism of the electorate essential, if a Labour
Government was ever again to control the British State. Whether
Hobsbawm intended it or not, his arguments were taken as
generally supportive of this view. He became 'Neil Kinnock's
favourite Marxist', and not surprisingly. For to those left-wingers
in the GLC and elsewhere who were so critical of Kinnock-style
moderation, the Hobsbawm voice by 1983 was arguing the case for
staying close to Labour's traditional supporters. He was writing
then that 'the working class has changed, the country has
changed . . . and unless Labour can become the party of the
working class it has no future, except as a coalition of minority
pressure groups and interests' (Hobsbawm 1983, p.10). But to
those traditional left-wingers within the Labour coalition who
were potentially empathetic to his critique of the excesses of the

'new movements' people, the Hobsbawm voice gave no quarter either. Even when Britain, as he reminded them, was overwhelmingly a 'country of manual workers . . . Labour marched forward by mobilising not only the proletariat as proletariat, but a wide coalition of forces'. For Hobsbawm that width was important too: for both the logic of class recombination within Late Capitalism (his 1978 concern) and of electoral disunity (his 1983 focus) combined to persuade him that Labour could not 'abandon its tradition of being a broad people's party . . . if Labour were to recover only the support of the manual working class,' he wrote in 1983, 'it would probably no longer be enough to give it victory, given the decline in its numbers and the rate of deindustrialisation' (ibid., p.10).

The Hobsbawm thesis thus set its face against too left-wing, or too workerist, a Labour Party, against one that 'established a correct position, and waited for the British people to recognise how wrong they are in not agreeing with it' (ibid., p.10). The emphasis of his writings focused on the need to come to terms with a more affluent, less politicised, and less class-conscious proletariat, one made up of 'men and women, blue collar, white collar and no collar, ranging from zero CSE to Ph.D, who are, regrettably, not revolutionaries, even though they want a new and better Britain' (Hobsbawm 1981, p.181). In his view:

> even the 'old' working class is no longer what it was a generation ago. . . . In general . . . mass support for political advance and the assertion of class consciousness have waned . . . Among elderly people I frequently find a sympathetic response and a clear class understanding in discussion. These are less strong in later generations, although many young people are evidently looking for a more radical alternative. . . . There have been changes that discourage the old type of political consciousness. Thus the values of consumer-society individualism and the search for private and personal satisfactions above all else, have been daily taken into every living room for a generation by the media. . . . Moreover the weakening of the hold of the old Labour movement itself has made some workers less resistant to reactionary infections such as racism. . . . The future of Labour and the advance to socialism depends on mobilising people who remember the date of the Beatles breakup and not the date of the Saltley picket.
>
> (ibid., pp.176 and 181)

The question, of course, is how to do this, how to win back such a proletariat to socialism. Hobsbawm's personal preference in

1983 was for a strategy close to that of the Italian Communist Party—one in which Labour 'rallies the widest range of forces around its essential core of the organised working class'—or, failing that, one in which the Labour Party will 'have to learn how to lead a broad front of other parties or their supporters into backing Labour policy' (Hobsbawm 1983, p.12). Hobsbawm has clearly been right to draw attention to the broad coalition of forces whose support is vital to the electoral success of any left-wing government, and to the exposure of that coalition over a long period to patterns of industrial development and social and cultural change that make its availability for socialist mobilisation more problematic than it has ever been. The Left is in a hole, as Hobsbawm continues to remind us; and, as always when in holes, the first trick is to stop digging.

Yet if we follow his line of argument, the Labour Party and its electorate are now drifting apart because of Labour Party radicalism, not Labour Party moderation. Radicalism within the Party now runs the danger of leaving broad sweeps of traditional Labour voters available to the Conservatives. Labour has therefore to go back, win them with policies geared to their immediate concerns and current self-definitions, and begin the process of subsequent radicalisation from a basis of a renewed unity between party and class of an initially moderate kind. This, of course, is quintessentially the Kinnock strategy for Labour's revival. It is, at worst, a tailoring of policy to existing levels of Thatcher-shaped consciousness. It is, at best, counter-hegemony by stealth. The question is: even at its best, is it enough?

IV

I think not, for a number of reasons. The first turns on the credibility of Labour's moderate alternative. There can be no going back to 1970s-style Keynesianism, for the simple reason that the political crisis which precipitated Thatcher into power was, as we saw, a crisis of the entire Labourist project. It was, at one and the same time, a crisis of Keynesianism, of corporatism, and of the

Labourist notion of public ownership. Governments in the 1970s could not spend their way out of stagflation, and still cannot. Governments in the 1970s could not negotiate the economy back to competitive strength through corporatist manoeuvres, and they still cannot. The social security system that the Attlee Government created has been used for too long as an agency of labour control, and has helped to perpetuate the poverty, to which it was itself a response, for too long now to be able alone to mobilise popular enthusiasm for the Labour Party. If the Labour Party tries to emphasise its moderation and its responsibility by toning down the radicalism of its programmes, it will neither persuade the marginal voter of its good intention nor inspire the activists to campaign with enthusiasm on its behalf. The Labour Party will need to create a *crusade* if it is to return to power; and that crusade will have to involve the development and propagation of policies equally radical to those of Thatcher, radical in a qualitatively different direction to hers. Labour needs a crusade against inequality, against unprincipled individualism, against the inadequacy of allocation and planning based solely on market forces, against dominant definitions of power blocs in international relations, and against the reactionary morality of the New Right. It will not launch that crusade by distancing itself from workers in struggle against the market, by toning down its policies on defence and disarmament, and by pandering to popular prejudices on sexuality and family self-reliance.

Labour will need to develop, if it is to succeed, its own long-term alternative strategy to set against Thatcherism. As Stuart Hall has correctly observed, 'what most distinguishes Thatcherism's wide-ranging conduct of ideological politics from Labour's narrow, tactical parliamentarianism, is exactly this unremitting attention to the long-term, strategic political "pay-off" of apparently short-term crises' (Hall 1988, p.20). The Thatcherite domination of deep underlying assumptions remains largely intact—the equation of the 'efficient' with the 'private', and of both with 'market forces' and 'individual freedom'. 'Thatcherite politics is inextricably ideological—it moulds people's conceptions as it restructures their lives as it shifts the disposition of forces to its side' (ibid., p.23).

The Left has to wage its own campaign at that deeper level, reasserting the validity of alternative socialist linkages between the public and the private, between individual needs and social responsibility, between economic equality and individual freedom. It has to match Thatcherism at the level of philosophy—developing a socialist philosophy to drown out a conservative one. That philosophy, if it is to be credible, will have to drown out social democracy too. It will have to include a left-wing critique of the limits of the post-war settlement to set against a Thatcherite reading of those limits. If the Left is to win back the electoral ground it has lost, it will have to recognise that it lost that ground for good reason; and be able to concede that bureaucratised public ownership, the mixed economy, and welfare provision of the Attlee kind do have problems.

It will also have to persuade many people that the resolution of those problems requires—not a retreat into privatisation, the market and individual self-interest—but an advance into a fuller and more egalitarian democratisation of economic and social life in Britain. And that persuasion will be the more effective the closer it models itself on the approach to ideological politics adopted by the Thatcherism it wishes to replace. For Thatcherism always operates through *code words*: 'greater efficiency' (meaning: reducing trade union power) or 'alternative sources of funding' (meaning: cutting back government support); and it deploys regularly its own *organising set of underlying themes*. Stuart Hall lists these as:

> The public sector is bureaucratic and inefficient; the private sector is efficient and gives 'value for money'; efficiency is inextricably linked with 'competition' and 'market forces'; the 'dependency culture' makes growing demands on the state—unless ruthlessly disciplined—a 'bottomless pit' (the spectre of the endlessly desiring consumer); public sector institutions, protected by public sector unions, are always 'overmanned' (sic); 'freedom' would be enhanced by giving the money back to the punters and letting them choose the form and level of health care they want; if there is money to spare, it is the direct result of 'Thatcherite prosperity' and so on. In short the familiar Thatcherite litany which is indelibly imprinted on the public mind and imposed on public and private discourse everywhere.
>
> (Hall 1988, pp.24–5)

The recognition of this Thatcherite way of working gives the Left two ideological jobs to do. One is to break the code words, exposing them for the sham they are. The other is to challenge at the level of underlying themes; and to impose a new set of socialist concerns—reappropriating the terminology Thatcherism has colonised—on democracy, freedom, responsibility and worth—and infusing them with a revitalised sense of the importance and appropriateness of socialist values of equality, comradeship and mutual support.

That is, of course, always easier said than done. The impact of Conservative thought runs so deep that such calls are often dismissed as utopian. But we must be careful, as we take stock, not to slide from realism to defeatism, or from pessimism to demoralisation. The forces that stand against the Left are always visible and powerful. Those which the Left wishes to mobilise are only immanent and untried. A stocktaking of what can easily be seen must, therefore, distort by virtue of its method. Radicals, precisely because they would have people change to a future whose promise cannot be guaranteed, are always burdened with the twin task of locating agencies of change, and clarifying goals, without the comfort of the legitimate order behind them, able to offer theory rather than history as their ultimate legitimating moment. The dangers of so 'unanchored' a basis for argument are clear: of an erratic oscillation between a mode of thought which is overwhelmed by immediate difficulties and one inspired by ungrounded flights of fancy. The rhythms of stocktaking on the Left have to move with Gramsci's instruction to follow 'pessimism of the intellect' with 'optimism of the will'. That stocktaking has always to be able to demonstrate that its hopes are more than utopian, its selection of agents more than idiosyncratic, and its assessment of problems and solutions linked and validated through some coherent understanding of the dynamics and contradictions of the existing order.

To my mind, what that understanding seems to suggest is that the British Left has no real choice in the 1990s but to go on the offensive both against Thatcher and against its own past. It will no longer 'sell' its old programme successfully. Nor can it offer a watered-down version of its opponents' programme without losing the remains of its credibility both with its Left and with its Right. It has an audience waiting for its revival in a new and radical form if it has the political courage to make so sharp a break with Labourism. It is time for confidence on the Left again, time to start arguing unapologetically for a radical recasting of ownership in industry and the extension of workers' rights, for a fundamental recasting of the way tasks are allocated and rewarded between classes, genders and ethnic groups in contemporary Britain, and for the total replacement of private welfare provision by adequate free state provision for all. The Left needs to start talking the language of class again, unashamedly asking workers to see themselves in that light, and urging them to defend their employment and their control of their work processes, against employer, government and courts alike.

This ideological struggle must be matched by a widening of political activity by the Left. Words and actions must fuse in a common defence of jobs, rights and human dignity. The Labour Party has to re-unite its bloc of classes into a radical coalition; and if the public sector Left is 'its' for want of any other political home, the manual working class in private industry is not. There the Labour Party needs to prove its credentials all over again; and can only do so by a full and unambiguous support for those workers in struggle. Time and again, workers in the Thatcher years have struck, looked for support elsewhere, tried to generalise their struggles, only to see the courts sequester their funds and the Labour politicians (with a few noble exceptions) absent themselves in silence. No regalvanisation of left-wing forces will come through that silence, or through the pretence of the neutrality between classes of a legal system now so set against effective working class resistance to managerial power. A galvanisation can come if, and to the degree that, a Labour leadership emerges willing to give unambiguous support to industrial challenges to that law, and unambiguous support to mass protests against attacks on civil rights in the areas of welfare, housing, sexuality and defence. If the Left is to regroup successfully in the 1990s, its political leadership will need to be both visible and radical industrially, socially and ideologically. The fear of short-term electoral losses needs to be replaced by the confidence of long-term socialist success, because only that confidence can create and mobilise the coalition of social forces which, in the immediate period, can unite defensively to protect jobs and rights and, in the longer term, can recapture state power in the service of a radical socialist project.

This study of the politics of industrial relations in contemporary Britain indicates how vital both a defensive and offensive bloc of social forces now is, and how available the social groups are which could constitute it. The existing political leadership of the Left has a clear opportunity. If it does not take it in the 1990s, the legacy of this century's labour movement in Britain to the labour movement of the next century will be sombre indeed.

Bibliography

Aaronovitch, S. *et al.* (1981) *The Political Economy of British Capitalism: a Marxist Analysis*, McGraw-Hill.

Ackrill, M. (1987) *Manufacturing Industry Since 1870*, Philip Allan.

Alt, J.(1979) *The Politics of Economic Decline*, Cambridge University Press.

Arnott, H. (1987) 'Second Class Citizens', in A.Walker and C.Walker (eds) *The Growing Divide: a Social Audit 1979–84*, Child Poverty Action Group, London, pp. 61–9.

Atkinson, J. (1984) 'Manpower strategies for flexible organisations', *Personnel Management*, August.

Bain, G.S. (1983) *Industrial Relations in Britain*, Basil Blackwell.

Barberis, P. (1987) *The Keynesian Revolution in Whitehall: An Assessment*, Manchester Polytechnic Occasional Papers in Social Science.

Barnes, D. and Reid, E. (1980) *Government and Trade Unions: the British Experience 1964–1979*, Heinemann.

Barnett, A. (1973) 'Heath, the Unions and the State: class struggle and the Heath Government', *New Left Review*, 77, pp. 3–41.

Barratt Brown, M. (1972) *From Labourism to Socialism*, Spokesman.

Bassell, P. (1986) *Strike-Free: New Industrial Relations in Britain*, Macmillan.

Batstone, E. *et al.* (1977) *Shop Stewards in Action*, Basil Blackwell.

Batstone, E. *et al.* (1987) *New Technology and the Process of Labour Regulation*, Oxford University Press.

Beaumont, P.B. (1987) *The Decline of Trade Union Organisation*, Croom Helm.

Beecham, D. (1981) 'Updating the downturn: class struggle under the Tories', *International Socialism*, 14, pp. 44–74.

Beechey, V. and Perkins, T. (1987) *A Matter of Hours: Women, Part-time Work and the Labour Market*, Polity Press.

Behrens, R. (1978) 'Blinkers for the carthorse: the Conservative Party and the trade unions 1974–78', *Political Quarterly*, vol. 49, pp. 457–66.

Benn, C. and Fairley, J. (eds) (1986) *Challenging the MSC: On Jobs, Education and Training*, Pluto.

Beynon, H. (ed.) (1985) *Digging Deeper: Issues in the Miners' Strike*, Verso.

Blackwell, R. and Terry, M. (1987) 'Analysing the Political Fund ballots: a remarkable victory or the triumph of the status quo?', *Political Studies*, vol. XXXV, pp. 623–42.

Blackwell, T. and Seabrook, J. (1985) *A World Still to Win: the Reconstruction of the Post-War Working Class*, Faber and Faber.

Booth, A. (1982) 'Corporatism, capitalism and depression in twentieth-century Britain', *British Journal of Sociology*, vol. 33 (2), pp. 200–23.

Boraston, I. *et al.* (1975) *Workplace and Union*, Heinemann.

Bornstein, S. and Gourevitch, P. (1984) 'Unions in a declining economy: the case of the British TUC', in P. Gourevitch *et al.*, *Unions and Economic Crisis*, Allen and Unwin, pp. 13–78.

Bright, D. *et al.* (1983) 'Industrial Relations in Recession', *Industrial Relations Journal*, vol. 14, pp. 24–33.

Brown, W. (1981) *The Changing Contours of British Industrial Relations*, Basil Blackwell.

Buckley, P.J. and Enderwick, P. (1985) *The Industrial Relations Practices of Foreign-Owned Firms in Britain*, Macmillan.

Burgess, K. (1980) *The Challenge of Labour*, Croom Helm.

Callinicoss, A. and Harman, C. (1987) *The Changing Working Class*, Bookmarks.

Campbell, J. *et al.* (1987) 'Symposium: the Thatcher years', *Contemporary Record*, vol. 1(3), pp. 34–43.

Clegg, H. (1969) 'The substance of productivity bargaining', in A. Flanders (ed.) *Collective Bargaining*, Penguin.

Clegg, H. and Flanders, A. (1954) *The System of Industrial Relations in Great Britain*, Basil Blackwell.

Cliff, T. *The Employers' Offensive*, Pluto.

Coates, D. (1972) *Teachers' Unions and Interest Group Politics*, Cambridge University Press.

Coates, D. (1975) *The Labour Party and the Struggle for Socialism*, Cambridge University Press.

Coates, D. (1980) *Labour in Power?* Longman.

Coates, D. (1983a) 'The question of trade union power', in D. Coates and G. Johnston (eds) *Socialist Arguments*, Martin Robertson.

Coates, D. (1983b) 'The Labour Party and the Future of the Left', in R. Miliband and J. Saville (eds) *The Socialist Register 1983*, Merlin, pp. 90–102.

Coates, D. (1984a) 'Corporatism and the State in theory and practice', in M. Harrison (ed.) *Corporatism and the Welfare State*, Gower, pp. 122–35.

Coates, D. (1984b) *The Context of British Politics*, Hutchinson.

Coates, D. (1985) *Modern Britain: Economic Crises*, Unit 8 of D102, Open University Foundation Course in the Social Sciences.

Coates, D. (1986) 'Social democracy and the logic of political traditions', *Economy and Society*, vol. 15 (3), pp. 414–25.

Coates, D. and Hillard, J. (eds) (1986) *The Economic Decline of Modern Britain*, Wheatsheaf.

Coates, D. and Hillard, J. (eds) (1987) *The Economic Revival of Modern Britain*, Edward Elgar.

Coates, K. (1982) 'The vagaries of participation 1945–1965', in B. Pimlott and C. Cook (eds) *Trade Unions in British Politics*, Longman.

Crewe, I. (1982) 'The Labour Party and the electorate', in D.Kavanagh (ed.) *The Politics of the Labour Party*, Allen and Unwin, pp. 9–49.

Crewe, I. (1986) 'On the death and resurrection of class voting: some comments on *How Britain Votes*', *Political Studies*, vol. XXXIV, pp. 620–38.

Crewe, I., Sarlvik, B. and Robertson, D. (1977) 'Partisan realignment in Britain 1964–74', *British Journal of Political Science*, vol. 7, pp. 129–90.

Crick, M. (1985) *Scargill and the Miners*, Penguin.

Cronin, J.E. (1984) *Labour and Society in Britain 1918–1979*, Batsford.

Crosland, C.A.R. (1956) *The Future of Socialism*, Cape.

Crosland, C.A.R. (1974) *Socialism Now; and Other Essays*, Cape.

Crouch, C. (1978) 'The intensification of industrial conflict in the UK', in C. Crouch and A.Pizzorno (eds) *The Resurgence of Class Conflict in Western Europe*, Macmillan.

Daniel, W.W. and Millward, N. (1983) *Workplace Industrial Relations in Britain*, Heinemann.

Davis, M. (1987) *Prisoners of the American Dream*, Verso.

Deakin, S. (1986) 'Labour law and the development of employment relationship in the UK', *Cambridge Journal of Economics*, vol. 10, pp. 225–46.

Dorfman, G.A. (1974) *Wage Politics in Britain 1945–1967*, Charles Knight.

Dorfman, G.A. (1979) *Government versus Trade Unionism in British Politics since 1968*, Macmillan.

Edgell, S. and Duke, V. (1986) 'Radicalism, radicalisation and recession: Britain in the 1980s', *British Journal of Sociology*, vol. XXXVII (4), pp. 479–512.

Edwards, P. (1982) 'Britain's changing strike problem', *Industrial Relations Journal*, vol. 13, pp. 5–20.

Elliott, J. (1978) *Conflict and Co-operation: the Growth of Industrial Democracy*, Kegan Paul.

England, J. and Weekes, B. (1981) 'Trade unions and the state: a review of the crisis', *Industrial Relations Journal*, vol. 12, pp. 10–26.

Engleman, S.R. and Thomson, A.W.J. (1974) 'Experience under the British Industrial Relations Act', *Industrial Relations*, vol. 13 (22), pp. 131–55.

Farnham, D. and Pimlott, J. (1986) *Understanding Industrial Relations*, Holt, Rinehart and Winston.

Fels, A. (1972) *The British Prices and Incomes Board*, Cambridge University Press.

Fine, B. and Miller, R. (eds) (1985) *Policing the Miners' Strike*, Lawrence and Wishart.

Flanders, A. (1964) *The Fawley Productivity Agreements*, Faber.

Flanders, A. (1970), *Management and Unions*, Faber.

Foot, M. (1962) *Aneurin Bevan: Volume 1, 1897–1945*, Four Square.

Fox, A. (1985) *History and Heritage*, Allen and Unwin

Friedman, A. (1977) *Industry and Labour: Class Struggle at Work and Monopoly Capitalism*, Macmillan.

Gabriel, Y. (1978) 'Collective bargaining: a critique of the Oxford school', *Political Quarterly*, vol. 49, pp. 334–48.

Gamble, A. (1979) 'The Free Economy and the Strong State', in R.Miliband and J. Saville (eds) *The Socialist Register 1979*, Merlin, pp. 1–25.

Geary, R. (1986) *Policing Industrial Disputes 1893–1985*, Methuen.

Glendinning, C. (1987) 'Impoverishing women', in A. Walker and C. Walker (eds) *The Growing Divide*, CPAG, pp. 50–60.

Goldthorpe, J. (1974) 'Industrial relations in Great Britain: a critique of reformism', reprinted from *Politics and Society* in T. Clarke and L. Clements (eds) (1977) *Trade Unions under Capitalism*, Fontana, pp. 184–224.

Goldthorpe, J., Lockwood, D., Bechhofer, F. and Platt, J. (1968–9) *The Affluent Worker* (in 3 volumes), Cambridge University Press.
    Volume 1: *Industrial Attitudes and Behaviour*
    Volume 2: *Political Attitudes and Behaviour*
    Volume 3: *The Affluent Worker in the Class Structure*

Goodman, J. (1975) 'Great Britain: towards the social contract', in S. Barkin (ed.) *Worker Militancy and its Consequences 1965–1975*, Praeger, pp. 39–80.

Goodman, J. and Whittingham, T. (1969) *Shop Stewards in British Industry*, McGraw-Hill.

Gough, I. (1983) 'Thatcherism and the welfare state', in S.Hall and M. Jacques (eds) *The Politics of Thatcherism*, Lawrence and Wishart, pp. 148–68.

Hall, S. (1982a) 'The battle for socialist ideas in the 1980s', in M. Eve and D. Musson (eds) *The Socialist Register 1982*, Merlin, pp. 1–20.

Hall, S. (1982b) 'The long haul', *Marxism Today*, November, pp. 16–21.

Hall, S. (1983) 'The Great Moving Right Show', in S.Hall and M.Jacques (eds) *The Politics of Thatcherism*, Lawrence and Wishart, pp. 19–39.

Hall, S. (1985) 'Authoritarian Populism: a reply', *New Left Review*, 151, May–June, pp. 115–24.

Hall, S. (1986) 'No light at the end of the tunnel', *Marxism Today*, December, pp. 12–16.

Hall, S. (1988) 'Thatcher's lessons', *Marxism Today*, March, pp. 20–27.

Hall, S. *et al.* (1978) *Policing the Crisis: Mugging, the State, and Law and Order*, Macmillan.

Hall, S. and Jacques, Martin (eds) (1983) *The Politics of Thatcherism*, Lawrence and Wishart.

Harman, C. (1986) 'The working class after the recession', *International Socialism*, vol. 33, pp. 3–33.

Hartley, J., Kelly, J. and Nicholson, N. (1983) *Steel Strike: A Case Study in Industrial Relations*, Batsford.

Hawkins, K. (1975) 'The miners and incomes policy 1972–75', *Industrial Relations Journal*, vol. 6 (2), pp. 4–22.

Heath, A. and MacDonald, S. (1987) 'Social change and the future of the Left', *Political Quarterly*, vol. 58 (4), pp. 364–77.

Hobsbawm, E. (1981) *The Forward March of Labour Halted*, Verso.

Hobsbawm, E. (1983) 'Labour's lost millions', *Marxism Today*, October, pp. 7–13.

Hughes, J. and Moore, R. (eds) (1972) *A Special Case? Social Justice and the Miners*, Penguin.

Hyman, R. (1972) *Strikes*, Fontana.

Hyman, R. (1973) 'Industrial conflict and the political economy', in R. Miliband and J. Saville (eds) *The Socialist Register 1973*, Merlin, pp. 101–54.

Hyman, R. (1975) *Industrial Relations: a Marxist Introduction*, Macmillan.

Hyman, R. (1978) 'Pluralism, procedural consensus and collective bargaining', *British Journal of Industrial Relations*, vol 16, pp. 16–40.

Hyman, R. (1979) 'The politics of workplace trade unionism: recent tendencies and some problems for theory', *Capital and Class*, 8, pp.54–67.

Hyman, R. (1980) 'British trade unionism: post-war trends and future prospects', *International Socialism*, vol. 2(8), pp. 66–79.

Hyman, R. (1983) 'Trade unions: structure, policies and politics', in G.S.Bain (ed.) *Industrial Relations in Britain*, Basil Blackwell, pp. 35–66.

Hyman, R. (1985) 'Class struggle and the trade union movement', in D. Coates, G. Johnston and R. Bush (eds) *A Socialist Anatomy of Britain*, Polity, pp. 99–123.

Hyman, R. (1986) 'Reflections on the mining strike', in R. Miliband and J. Saville (eds) *The Socialist Register 1985–6*, Merlin, pp. 330–54.

Hyman, R. (1987) 'Trade unions and the law: papering over the cracks', *Capital and Class*, 31, pp. 93–113.

Hyman, R. (1988), *The Political Economy of Industrial Relations*, Macmillan.

Hyman, R. and Elger, T. (1981) 'Job controls, the employers' offensive and alternative strategies', *Capital and Class*, 15, pp. 114–49.

Hyman, R. and Fryer, B. (1974) 'Trade unions: sociology and political economy', in J. McKinlay (ed.) *Processing People*, Holt-Blond, pp. 150–213.

Jackson, M. (1987) *Strikes: Industrial Conflict in Britain, USA and Australia*, Wheatsheaf.

Jacques, M. (1987) 'Close to the heart of our life and times', *Guardian*, 14.12.1987, p.10.

Jeffries, S. (1979) 'Striking into the 1980s: modern trade unionism—its limits and potential', *International Socialism*, vol. 5, Summer, pp. 1–53.

Jenkins, P. (1970) *The Battle of Downing Street*, Charles Knight.

Jessop, B. (1983) 'The democratic state and the national interest', in D. Coates and G. Johnston (eds) *Socialist Arguments*, Martin Robertson, pp. 83–106.

Jessop, B. (1988) 'Conservative regimes and the transition to post-Fordism: the cases of Britain and West Germany', *Essex Papers in Politics and Government*, Department of Government, University of Essex.

Jessop, B. *et al.* (1984) 'Authoritarian Populism, Two Nations and Thatcherism', *New Left Review*, 147, September–October, pp. 32–60.

Johnson, P. (1975) 'A brotherhood of national misery', *New Statesman*, 16.5.1975, pp. 652–5.

Joseph, Sir Keith (1978) *Conditions for Full Employment*, Centre for Policy Studies, London.

Joseph, Sir Keith (1979) *Solving the Union Problem is the Key to Britain's Recovery*, Centre for Policy Studies, London.

Kavanagh, D. (ed.) (1982) *The Politics of the Labour Party*, Allen and Unwin.

Kavanagh, D. (1985) 'Whatever happened to consensus politics?', *Political Studies*, vol. XXXIII, pp. 529–46.

Keynes, J.M. (1936) *The General Theory of Employment, Interest and Money*, Macmillan.

Krieger, J. (1986) *Reagan, Thatcher and the Politics of Decline*, Polity.

Leopold, J.W. (1986) 'Trade union political funds: a retrospective analysis', *Industrial Relations Journal*, vol. 17, pp. 287–303.

Lewis, R. (1983) 'Collective labour law', in G.S.Bain (ed.) *Industrial Relations in Britain*, Basil Blackwell, pp. 367–92.

Lipset, S.M. (1960) *Political Man*, Mercury.

Lockwood, D. (1975) 'Sources of variation in working class images of society', in M. Bulmer (ed.) *Working Class Images of Society*, Routledge and Kegan Paul, pp. 16–34.

Longstreth, F.H. (1988) 'From corporatism to dualism: Thatcherism and the climacteric of British Trade Unions in the 1980s', *Political Studies*, vol. XXXVI (3), pp.413–32. (Page references cited in the text refer to unpublished MS version.)

Looker, R.J. and Coates, D. (1983) 'Basic problems of socialist strategy', in D. Coates and G. Johnston (eds) *Socialist Strategies*, Martin Robertson, pp. 241–82.

MacInnes, J. (1985) 'Conjuring up consultation: the role and extent of joint consultation in post-war private manufacturing industry', *British Journal of Industrial Relations*, vol. 23.

MacInnes, J. (1987) *Thatcherism at Work: Industrial Relations and Economic Change*, Open University Press.

McIlroy, J. (1985a) 'Police and pickets: the law against the miners', in H. Beynon (ed.) *Digging Deeper*, Verso, pp. 107–22.

McIlroy, J. (1985b) 'The law struck dumb—labour law and the miners' strike', in B. Fine and R. Miller (eds) *Policing and the Miners' Strike*, Lawrence and Wishart, pp. 79–102.

Marsh, D. and King, J. (1985) 'The Trade Unions under Thatcher', *Essex Papers in Politics and Government*, No. 27, Department of Government, University of Essex.

Marsh, D. and Locksley, G. (1981) 'Trade union power in Britain: the recent debate', *West European Politics*, vol 4, pp. 19–37.

McCarthy, W. (1966) *The Role of Shop Stewards in British Industrial Relations*, Research Paper No. 1 to the Royal Commission on Trade Unions and Employers Associations, HMSO.

McCarthy, W. (ed.) (1972) *Trade Unions*, Penguin.

Marshall, G. *et al.* (1985) 'Class, citizenship and distributional conflict in modern Britain', *British Journal of Sociology*, vol. XXXVI, pp. 259–84.

Massey, D. (1983) 'The shape of things to come', *Marxism Today*, April pp. 18–27.

Middlemas, K. (1979) *Politics in Industrial Society*, Deutsch.

Middlemas, K. (1983) *Industry, Unions and Government: 21 Years of the NEDC*, Macmillan.

Millward, N. and Stevens, M. (1985) *British Workplace Industrial Relations*, Gower.

Minkin, L. (1978) 'The Labour Party has not been hijacked', *New Society*, 6.10.1975, pp. 7–9.

Mitchell, N. (1987a) 'Where traditional Tories fear to tread: Mrs. Thatcher's trade union policy', *West European Politics*, vol. 10(1), pp. 33–45.

Mitchell, N. (1987b) 'Changing pressure group politics; the case of the TUC, 1976–1984', *British Journal of Political Science*, vol. 17, pp. 509–17.

Mouffe, C. (1980) 'Hegemony and the integral state in Gramsci: towards a new concept of politics', in G. Bridges and R. Brunt (eds) *Silver Linings*, Lawrence and Wishart.

Nichols, T. (1987) *The British Worker Question: a New Look at Workers and Productivity in Manufacturing*, Routledge and Kegan Paul.

Palmer, G. (1986) 'Donovan, the Commission on Industrial Relations, and post-liberal rationalisation', *British Journal of Industrial Relations*, vol. 24(2), pp. 267–96.

Panitch, L. (1976) *Social Democracy and Industrial Militancy*, Cambridge University Press.

Panitch, L. (1986) *Working Class Politics in Crisis*, Verso.

Panitch, L. (1988) 'Socialist renewal and the Labour Party', in R. Miliband, L. Panitch and J. Saville (eds) *The Socialist Register 1988*, Merlin, pp. 319–65.

Parkin, F. (1966) 'Working class Conservatives: a theory of political deviance', *British Journal of Sociology*, vol. 18(4), pp. 278–90.

Piachaud, D. (1987) 'The growth of poverty', in A. Walker and C.Walker (eds) *The Growing Divide*, CPAG, London, pp. 20–6.

Pimlott, B. and Cook, C. (eds) (1982) *Trade Unions in British Politics*, Longman.

Poole, M. (1986) *Industrial Relations*, Routledge and Kegan Paul.

Poole, M. *et al.* (1984) *Industrial Relations in the Future: Trends and Possibilities in Britain Over the Next Decade*, Routledge and Kegan Paul.

Price, R. and Bain, G.S. (1976) 'Union growth revisited: 1948–1974 in perspective', *British Journal of Industrial Relations*, vol. XIV(3), pp. 339–55.

Price, R. and Bain, G.S. (1983) 'Union growth in Britain: retrospect and prospect', *British Journal of Industrial Relations*, vol. XXI, pp. 46–68.

Przeworski, A. (1985) *Capitalism and Social Democracy*, Cambridge University Press.

Purcell, J. (1979) 'The lessons of the Commission on Industrial Relations: attempts to reform workplace industrial relations', *Industrial Relations Journal*, vol. 10, pp. 4–22.

Purcell, J. and Sissons, K. (1983) 'Strategies and practice in the management of industrial relations' in G.S. Bain (ed.) *Industrial Relations in Britain*, Basil Blackwell, pp. 95–120.

Riddell, P. (1983) *The Thatcher Government*, Martin Robertson.

Robertson, D. (1984) 'Adversary politics, public opinion and electoral cleavages', in D. Kavanagh and G. Peele (eds) *Comparative Government and Politics*, Heinemann.

Rubery, J. (1986) 'Trade unions in the 1980s: the case of the United Kingdom', in R. Edwards *et al.* (eds) *Unions in Crisis and Beyond*, Auburn House, Dover, Mass.

Rubery, J. and Tarling, R. (1988) 'Women's employment in declining Britain', in J. Rubery (ed.) *Women and Recession*, Routledge and Kegan Paul, pp. 100–32.

Saville, J. (1967) 'Labourism and the Labour Government', in R. Miliband and J. Saville (eds) *The Socialist Register 1967*, Merlin, pp. 43–72.

Saville, J. (1973) 'The ideology of Labourism', in R. Benewick *et al.* (eds) *Knowledge and Belief in Politics*, Allen and Unwin, pp. 213–26.

Saville, J. (1986) 'An open conspiracy: Conservative politics and the miners' strike', in R. Miliband and J. Saville (eds) *The Socialist Register 1985–6*, Merlin, pp. 295–329.

Schmitter, P.C. (1974) 'Still the century of corporatism', *The Review of Politics*, vol. 36(1), pp. 85–131.

Schoer, K. (1987) 'Part-time employment: Britain and West Germany', *Cambridge Journal of Economics*, vol. 11, pp. 83–94.

Schwarz, B. (1987) 'The Thatcher years', in R. Miliband, L. Panitch and J. Saville (eds) *The Socialist Register 1987*, Merlin, pp. 116–55.

Sisson, K. and Brown, W. (1983) 'Industrial relations in the private sector: Donovan revisited', in G.S. Bain (ed.) *Industrial Relations in Britain*, Basil Blackwell. pp. 137–54.

Sivanandan, A. (1982) *A Different Hunger: Writings on Black Resistance*, Pluto.

Smith, T. (1979) *The Politics of the Corporate Economy*, Martin Robertson.

Solomos, J. (1985) 'Extended review: youth training, unemployment and state policies', *Sociological Review*, pp. 342–53.

Soskice, D. (1984) 'Industrial relations and the British economy 1979–1983', *Industrial Relations*, vol. 23, pp. 308–22.

Steele, M. *et al.* (1986) 'The Trade Union Act 1984: political fund ballots', *British Journal of Industrial Relations*, vol. 24(3), pp. 443–67.

Strinati, D. (1983) 'State intervention, the economy and the crisis: corporatism, radical conservatism and the state in Britain', in A. Stewart (ed.) *Contemporary Britain*, Routledge and Kegan Paul, pp. 41–93.

Tawney, R.H. (1932) 'The choice before the Labour Party', *Political Quarterly*, vol. 3.

Taylor, R. (1980) *The Fifth Estate: British Unions and the Modern World*, Pan.

Taylor, R. (1982) 'The trade union problem since 1960', in B. Pimlott and C. Cook (eds) *Trade Unions in British Politics*, Longman, pp. 188–214.

Taylor, R. (1987a) 'Trade unions and the Labour Party: time for an open marriage', *Political Quarterly*, vol. 58(4), pp. 424–32.

Taylor, R. (1987b) 'Trade unions since 1979', *Contemporary Record*, vol. 1(3), pp. 20–3.

Terry, M. (1983) 'Shop steward development and managerial strategies', in G.S.Bain (ed.) *Industrial Relations in Britain*, Basil Blackwell, pp. 67–94.

Terry, M. (1985) 'Combined committees: developments of the 1970s', *British Journal of Industrial Relations*, vol. 23(3), pp. 359–78.

Thompson, E.P. (1980) *Writing By Candlelight*, Merlin.

Tomlinson, J. (1984) *Employment Policy: the Crucial Years 1939–1955*, Clarendon Press.

Topham, T. (1969) 'Productivity Bargaining', in K. Coates *et al.* (eds) *Trade Union Register*, Merlin, pp. 68–95.

Volker, D. (1966) 'NALGO's affiliation to the TUC', *British Journal of Industrial Relations*, vol. 4, pp. 59–76.

Wainwright, H. (1987) *Labour: A Tale of Two Parties*, The Hogarth Press.

Walby, S. (1983) 'Women's unemployment, patriarchy and capitalism', in M. Sawyer and K. Schott (eds) *Socialist Economic Review 1983*, Merlin, pp. 99–114.

Walker, A. and Walker, C. (eds) (1987) *The Growing Divide: a Social Audit 1979–1987*, Child Poverty Action Group, London.

Watson, T. (1980) *Sociology, Work and Industry*, Routledge and Kegan Paul.

Webb, P. (1987) 'Union, party and class in Britain: the changing electoral relationship 1964–1983', *Politics*, vol. 8(7), pp. 15–21.

Westergaard, J. (1970) 'The rediscovery of the cash nexus', in R. Miliband and J. Saville (eds) *The Socialist Register 1970*, Merlin, pp. 111–38.

Willman, P. (1981) 'The growth of combined committees; a reconsideration', *British Journal of Industrial Relations*, vol. 19, pp. 1–13.

Willman, P. (1984) 'The reform of collective bargaining and strike activity in BL cars 1976–1982', *Industrial Relations Journal*, vol. 15, pp. 6–17.

Winchester, D. (1981) 'Trade unions and the recession', *Marxism Today*, September, pp. 20–25.

Winchester, D. (1983) 'Industrial relations in the public sector', in G.S.Bain (ed.) *Industrial Relations in Britain*, Basil Blackwell, pp. 155–78.

Winyard, S. (1987) 'Divided Britain', in A. Walker and C. Walker (eds) *The Growing Divide*, CPAG, London, pp. 39–49.

Wolfe, J. (1986), 'Class formation and democracy: the decline of working class power in Britain', *West European Politics*, vol. 9(3), pp. 343–61.

Index

DATE DUE			

Coates   223541